"As Prime Minister, I Would..."

"As Prime Minister, I Would..."

CANADA'S BRIGHTEST

OFFER

INNOVATIVE SOLUTIONS

FOR A MORE

PROSPEROUS AND UNITED

COUNTRY

FOREWORD BY FRANK STRONACH

KEY PORTER BOOKS

JUN 5 '96

Canadian Cataloguing in Publication Data

Main entry under title:

"As prime minister, I would ..."

ISBN 1-55013-729-X (bound)   ISBN 1-55013-731-X (pbk.)

1. Canada — Politics and government — 1993–   .*
2. Canada — Social policy. 3. Canada — Economic
policy — 1991–   .* I. Stronach, Frank.

FC635.A72 1995   971.064'8   C95-932549-2
F1034.2.A72 1995

Photo credits: Garry Boland Studio Production Ltd., p. 159; Harvey Studios, p. 97; Lane's Studio Photography, p. 211; Michael Bedford Photography, p. 149; Bret Newsome, p. 165; Rockcliffe Photo Image Centre, p. 27; Sesar Studio, p. 61; Studio Donald Portraitiste, p. 181

The publisher gratefully acknowledges the assistance of the Canada Council, the Ontario Arts Council and the Ontario Publishing Centre.

Key Porter Books
70 The Esplanade
Toronto, Ontario
Canada   M5E 1R2

Design: Heidi Palfrey
Printed and bound in Canada

95 96 97 98 99   5 4 3 2 1

CONTENTS

ACKNOWLEDGMENTS

The world is full of critics, and there are plenty of people who have opinions. But there are very few people who have solutions and the courage to submit those ideas to public scrutiny.

We salute the students and the other writers for their participation in this program and their courage in searching for solutions. They have done so in the spirit of serving their country, so that all Canadians might benefit from their ideas.

Frank Stronach

MAGNA FOR CANADA SCHOLARSHIP FUND ACKNOWLEDGMENTS

The sponsors of the Magna for Canada Scholarship Fund wish to acknowledge the contributions of the following people:

The Co-Chairs: Dennis Mills and Belinda Stronach

The Board of Governors: Michael Burns, Michelle Gervais, Elizabeth Parr-Johnston, John Oakley, Robert Pritchard, and Royden Richardson

The Judges: Patrick Boyer, Michael Burns, William Chabassol, Monique Jérome-Forget, Wade MacLauchlan, Jim Nicol, John Oakley, Hugh Segal, and Jack Webster

All the students from across Canada who submitted proposals and, in particular, those recognized below for *Honourable Mention*:

Nicole Cervenka, Elaine Curran, Craig Forcese, Michael Friedman, John Haffner, Byron Horner, Michael Hyatt, Christina Litz, Steven Lofkrantz, Kristi Nielsen, Stephen Penner, Damian Rogers, Jean-Marc Thibault, Stella Varvis, Darren Watts, Allison Young.

MAGNA FOR CANADA SCHOLARSHIP AWARDS PROGRAM JUDGING PROCESS

The winning student proposals contained in this book were selected by an independent and distinguished national panel of judges representing the different regions of the country. The panel was comprised of judges with backgrounds in business, academia, media, and government affairs.

The national panel of judges travelled across Canada to meet with more than eighty students whose papers were deemed to be among the best submissions received by the Scholarship Fund. Each student gave an oral synopsis of his or her proposal and was then interviewed by the panel.

The judges selected as the ten Regional Winners students whose proposals contained the most innovative and workable solutions and students who demonstrated a high degree of poise, knowledge, and skill during the interview sessions.

One of the ten Regional Winners will be declared the National Champion at an event taking place subsequent to the publication of this book. The National Champion will be identified in a publication to be produced the following year.

Disclaimer

FOREWORD

MOST CANADIANS KNOW THAT WE ARE BESIEGED BY A number of serious problems — we can feel it in our bones — everything from mounting debt and high unemployment to a deterioration of our living standards.

Canadians have a choice: we can either remain deadlocked in the current political framework, which we all know does not work, or we can embark upon a program of real reform and embrace a new vision of Canada. In seeking a source for that new vision, it is only natural that we look to our youth, who represent the future.

Herein lies the inspiration behind the Magna for Canada Scholarship Awards program, a national program designed to solicit from our college and university students innovative ways to improve Canadian living standards and unify the country. The very best proposals put forth by students from across the country are contained in this book. The scholarship awards program also solicited proposals from a number of distinguished Canadians in the fields of business, the arts, academia, and labour. The proposals of the students and contributing writers are heartfelt, insightful, and provocative. It is our hope that they will find their way to the surface of public discourse; that they will stir debate not only in the corridors of power but also in small-town coffee shops and university courtyards.

The Pursuit of Economic Freedom

I firmly believe that before we engage in discussion about the problems confronting our society we, as a nation, must have a clear vision of what would constitute an ideal society.

11

We must begin by attempting to understand the hopes, dreams, and aspirations of individuals. I feel strongly that most people have two very basic desires: first, they want to have personal freedom, which, in essence, means they want the right to choose their own road to happiness; and second, they want economic freedom, which really boils down to financial independence.

The reality is that people are not really free unless they have economic freedom. Economic freedom does not come easily. It is arrived at by hard work and good planning. And we need to recognize that governments cannot bestow economic freedom — governments can only give you what they have first taken from you. The role of government is not only to ensure law and order and freedom for its citizens, but also to ensure that everyone has an opportunity to become economically free. It is unfortunate that in our society very few people have attained this goal.

But what does economic freedom mean, and if it is so desirable, how can we achieve it? Ideally, the average Canadian should attain economic freedom after fifteen or twenty years of work. During that time, the average person should be able to save enough money to retire and live a modest life using the interest on his accumulated capital. That person would then be free to nourish his mind, heart, and soul by pursuing other activities, such as painting, gardening, volunteering for charitable causes or other meaningful endeavours. In the final analysis, success in life can only be measured by the degree of happiness you achieve.

We must ask ourselves, then, why are so few Canadians able to achieve economic freedom? Having arrived in this country with a limited education and barely any money, why was I able to achieve economic freedom? And, perhaps more importantly, if I were to arrive on these shores today and start all over again, would I be able to attain economic freedom? The truth is, it would be much more difficult.

This grim reality worries a lot of young Canadians, who harbour the same hopes, dreams, and ambitions I did. They worry that their homeland is no longer a land of opportunity. They are more concerned about economic survival than economic freedom.

Priorities of Government Reform

As the founder and Chairman of Magna International, business and personal reasons require me to spend most of my time in Europe, where we are currently undergoing a major expansion. But I still have a great concern for Canada. This country has been very good to me. Canadians are among the most generous and tolerant people in the world. Yet I worry that we have unwittingly travelled too far down the road of state enterprise and government control. We have allowed ourselves to get sucked into a system that stifles individual initiative and chokes the productive and economic activities of our country. Our country has major problems, and problems never go away on their own. Unless we pinpoint the problems and take aggressive action to solve them, they will only increase in severity.

The root of our problems, I believe, lies in the way in which we govern our country. Government is really the management team of a country, and the citizens of Canada are its shareholders. Unfortunately, our government management team is comprised of politicians whose first mandate is to be elected or re-elected. The result is that our country is managed mainly for political instead of economic considerations.

If I had to prioritize what we as a nation should do to improve our living standards, the first item on my agenda would be to reform our government management structure. As we all know, politics is unavoidable in a free society. But as long as Parliament is dominated by party politics, this country will always be driven by a political rather than an economic agenda. Because the well-being of a nation ultimately depends upon the strength of its economic fabric, the challenge we face is this: how can we ensure that the management decisions of government are also driven by economics? In other words, what can we do to create a framework or system that will balance the political decision-making process with an economic decision-making process?

I believe we need to abolish the Senate and replace it with a new chamber of democratically elected citizens. These new citizen members would be people elected by their fellow voters from a list of candidates chosen randomly, similar to the way we select juries. Citizen representatives would hold the balance of power under this new arrangement, thereby depoliticizing our Parliament. Because they could only serve for one term and would vote in secret, these new representatives would be much more inclined to place the country's economic welfare and long-term national interests ahead of political objectives or partisan views. But if the country's agenda continues to be driven by political concerns, then Canada will continue to falter.

When living standards deteriorate in a country, segments of society become frustrated because they feel stifled and dominated. I believe this explains to some extent the recent rekindling of separatist views in Quebec and growing disenchantment in other regions of the country. If Canada had its economic house in good order, then I believe there would not be a unity problem. The best assurance for the provinces to remain within the Canadian federation is the creation of a healthy economic climate for all Canadians.

Our Tax System

Our tax system has the greatest bearing on our living standards. As it presently exists, it is not geared towards the creation of wealth. More and more capital is being sucked out of the financial markets and into the hands of governments. In essence, we have created an environment in which we no longer reward those who take business risks. Our tax system has degenerated into a system that offers greater rewards to those who purchase government bonds than to those who run the risk of investing in private enterprise.

Most Canadians would agree: the tax system needs to be completely overhauled. We need to make it much simpler and easier to understand. And we need to make it more efficient. A flat tax, or a sales and consumption tax, would be much fairer and simpler, and would require only a fraction of the present government bureaucracy to administer.

Education

Our education system is another area that needs reform. We are not training and educating our students for the realities of today's workplace. We especially need to begin teaching our children how important business is to this country and to the maintenance of our standard of living. We need to realize that preserving a healthy business climate is as important as preserving the environment or social programs, because, in the final analysis, it is business that pays the bills for all of the social programs and amenities we enjoy.

Students must also realize that it is business that will create the majority of jobs, and that the real key to prosperity and job security lies in being globally competitive.

Government Overhead and Spending

Finally, we must make government more efficient, because the costs of running this country are simply too high. Government spending has gone way out of line. To put it plainly, we are too fat.

We need to begin by reducing government overhead and dismantling our massive bureaucratic framework. It could be done by eliminating waste and by gradually phasing out unnecessary services. And it could be done in a civilized way, without taking a chainsaw to the bureaucracy, and by providing generous severance packages to those who would be affected by the downsizing.

We must refrain from making bureaucrats, or any other segment of society, the scapegoats for our economic problems. Because of the prevailing passive attitude in this country, Canadians as a whole are to blame for Canada's economic problems. We as Canadians must become more involved and informed about our country. Canada cannot function effectively without the participation of all its citizens.

In short, we have to rethink and restructure the way in which government works. The most important reason for this is not simply to cut costs but to eliminate the red tape and bureaucratic roadblocks — the quiet killers of jobs and businesses.

I also believe it is the duty of every democracy to reaffirm the minimum standards of a civilized society. In a civilized society, every citizen should have access to health care, food, and shelter. We in Canada must re-examine our social programs in order to make them more efficient. If you have the means to pay for services such as education and health, then you should pay your fair share. In other words, the universality of our social programs needs to be redesigned.

New Directions

Our society has come a long way in promoting and protecting the democratic rights and freedoms enshrined in our Charter — and we must stand on guard to preserve these cherished principles. But at the same time our society has been so preoccupied with engineering social equality and redistributing wealth that we have neglected how to go about *creating* wealth. Any society that stifles individual initiative in the pursuit of excellence is a decaying society.

Canada has travelled fairly far down the road of wealth redistribution and state enterprise, but we know now that the socialistic approach does not work. In my business travels through Russia and parts of Eastern Europe I have seen firsthand the decay and poverty that state enterprise has brought to many countries.

Most politicians, business people, labour leaders and social activists are concerned about improving this country's living standards. But which road do we take? I am a great believer that we must do everything possible to preserve our free enterprise system. Without free enterprise, there is no free society. Yet I also realize that, from time to time, the free enterprise system, when in the grip of unbridled greed, can become self-destructive. I believe that free enterprise, co-existent with "fair enterprise," is the most beneficial system for a society. The basic philosophy behind "fair enterprise" is that our human charters of rights need to be fortified with economic charters of rights. Economic charters of rights would lead to an economic democracy, and economic democracies are the basis for democracy itself.

How Does "Fair Enterprise" Work in Practice?

A business that had an economic charter of rights would operate under "fair enterprise" principles and would have open books; its employees would get a portion of the profits and ownership in the company; and most of the company's profits would be reinvested in our country. If businesses operating under "fair enterprise" principles paid a lower tax rate, then more and more businesses would adopt these principles, and more and more Canadian employees would begin to feel that they had a stake not only in their place of employment but in their country as well. We would see an increase in productivity, a greater concern for our economic well-being, and a much fairer and broader distribution of wealth. Our whole economy — our whole country — would blossom and bloom.

If Canada were to enact changes of the sort I have mentioned — if we depoliticized our Parliament, cut the fat out of government, revamped our tax system, and adopted "fair enterprise" principles —

16

then we could transform Canada from a country burdened by excessive bureaucracy and high debt into one of the most progressive and prosperous nations in the world.

Frank Stronach
September 1995
Toronto

ONE

CHANGING THE MIND-SET: A NEW COURSE FOR CANADA

• • • • • • • • • •

JAMES WIEDRICK

After graduating with a Bachelor of Science degree in Pharmacy in 1993, James worked for two years in hospital and community pharmacies in both Edmonton and his hometown of Grimshaw, Alberta. He decided to pursue a career as a doctor and is currently enrolled in his second year in the Faculty of Medicine at the University of Alberta in Edmonton. James is the Faculty of Medicine's representative on the university Students' Union council and a member of the Medical Students' Association. He is an active golfer and curler and enjoys reading mysteries.

CANADA. I BELIEVE IT IS THE BEST COUNTRY IN THE WORLD in which to live. Canadians are keenly aware that we have the privilege of living in a modern democracy with abundant natural beauty and space. Yet most of us realize that Canada falls short when judged by its standard of living and sense of national unity. What, then, should we as a collective society do? As prime minister, I would offer a series of ideas and proposals to invigorate and renew our nation and help it to achieve greatness in the next millennium.

To do this effectively, the leader of Canada must present a clear, focused vision for the nation that all citizens can comprehend and support. As prime minister, my first step to achieving long-lasting unity and improved living standards would be to enact a paradigm shift, a change in the way we think and operate in this nation. We need to change the patterns and models for our nation's institutions and our way of thinking of ourselves. In many ways, our society is too dependent on government to fulfil personal needs and desires. We have become a society of victims, and this attitude of victimization constrains us. As Louis W. Sullivan has said: "To teach young people that their lives are governed — not by their own actions but by socioeconomic forces or government budgets or other mysterious and fiendish forces beyond their control — is to teach our children negativism, passivity, resignation and despair."

I fear that in Canada today we have instilled this type of attitude, especially among our youth, tomorrow's leaders. For future success as a nation we must break out of this mind-set, with the prime minister leading the way. All citizens of this country need to establish a spirit of independence and resolve, while working together with renewed vigour. Everything that we do as individuals, and as a federal government that works for these individuals, needs to be in the pursuit of national goals, with less reliance on national institutions. Let me elaborate.

As one of the components of the paradigm shift I propose, I would work as prime minister to foster unity by changing Canadians' perspective on themselves. First, Canadians must reach a new level of patriotism. We must make rallying points of our uniquely Canadian symbols, such as the flag. Few people know how the maple leaf came to be a national symbol, yet there is a tradition of at least 160 years behind it. Both French and English segments of society have used it proudly, both pre- and post-Confederation. As the prime minister I would educate society about our national symbols, use them more often, and use them with more pride.

More dramatically, I propose that we should establish Canada as a democratic republic. The Queen should no longer be head of state. While we should acknowledge the pivotal role that ties with Great Britain and the monarchy have played in our development as a country, Canadians must know and be proud of the fact that Canada stands on its own to face the world. In my view, our nation's unity can only be enhanced by such a move. The status quo hinders our future psychological development as a nation. Most Canadians no longer accept that we should be subjugated under British authority, symbolic or not. As prime minister, I would propose that a Canadian be selected by Parliament, much as the Speaker of the House is elected, to be the Canadian head of state, with prescribed duties that would be ceremonial in nature.

At the same time we must eliminate the trend towards hyphenated-Canadianism — that is, describing ourselves or our neighbours as French-Canadian, Ukrainian-Canadian, Korean-Canadian, or by whatever moniker their heritage may dictate. It is a fact that Canada is composed of people who were born, or whose ancestors were born, in other nations. However, citizens of this land should all be Canadian, period. To apply labels otherwise is only to divide or highlight differences. No matter where we came from, we are all Canadians now.

As prime minister I would apply this type of thinking to all my dealings and I would eliminate government-sponsored multiculturalism. The money and bureaucracy devoted therein should be redirected. Of course, individuals or groups must be able to, on their own initiative, recognize and celebrate their diverse backgrounds and heritages in an open and tolerant society. There is, however, no role for government here except to reinforce the Canadian culture. We must always be Canadian first and foremost.

Under my leadership, the government would not be in the business of social engineering. The Charter of Rights and Freedoms dictates that all Canadians are equal "before and under the law." Unfortunately, modern society's emphasis on ethnicity and individual labels only reinforces differences. We must not make the futile attempt to eliminate all bureaucratically perceived inequalities in our society through affirmative action programs and the like. Canadian society under my prime ministership would live by the credo of tolerance and equality before the law for all. Reverse discrimination is only a recipe for perpetuating hatred or envy. Instead, I believe in the underlying goodness of man and, with raised levels of social consciousness, society's ability to correct inequalities.

The second component of my proposed paradigm shift is the need for Canada to refine the national system for decision-making so that unity and an improved standard of living can be achieved. I would support as prime minister the immediate enactment of three items to enhance the role of citizens in the decision-making processes of government: termination of government funding of special-interest lobby groups, revamping of the system of parliamentary party discipline, and elimination of the Senate.

If a movement is worth sustaining, then it will be sustained by people, by individual citizens. It seems ironic that government, in an attempt to help citizens, takes power away from them by paying organizations to lobby and influence the government's decision-making. Ordinary citizens outside of federally supported lobby groups are bitter about the influence these groups have on government decisions. The money allocated here could be better spent on the initiatives I will discuss later.

As a complementary measure to give citizens a voice in government, we need to address House of Commons voting procedures and eliminate the unwritten rule that members of the ruling party must always support government initiatives. Members of Parliament must be allowed to and should vote according to their constituents' wishes. The current practice of strict party discipline severely limits the power of members of Parliament who are not in the cabinet and who do not have an opportunity to be involved in executive decision-making. As prime minister, I would initiate a fundamental change to bring back true representative democracy and allow members to speak out and vote against government positions if the wishes of their constituents dictated such action. Only on votes of confidence would I demand discipline.

Concurrently, the Senate, in the absence of substantial reforms, should be abolished. Certainly some expense will be spared the taxpayer. Perhaps more importantly, the symbolism of eliminating a do-nothing institution whose usefulness has been far outlived would encourage Canadians and give them renewed vigour and optimism about the powers-that-be.

As a final thought regarding our governance, I would oppose the creation of native self-government. Canada should prevent the degradation of federal authority and the further creation of another layer of government. Natives should not be exempt from any federal legislation, but should instead work for reform within the federal system. Canada must remain one nation, with one set of laws for all citizens.

As prime minister, I would work on another component of the paradigm shift: reducing our nation's dependence on government. I would identify a few key priorities for government and reinforce the federal role in those areas. However, in many other realms I would act to minimize the role of government. Standard of living, and ultimately unity, depend on the fiscal stability of the nation's government. Fiscal responsibility would be a key priority.

To help reduce federal deficits and debt, a slogan is worth keeping in mind: "Take care of the millions and the billions will take care of themselves." Along this line, it would be a strict rule of my leadership that government should not be in the business of manipulating economic forces. In the 1994–95 federal budget, $3.8 billion was allocated to the area of subsidies and transfers to businesses. Subsidies and tax breaks to corporations, whether big or small, would be eliminated if I were leader of the country. If a project or business cannot be successfully operated privately, it should not exist.

Concurrently, the economic balkanization of the country occurring via interprovincial trade barriers must be stopped. A free country must have free trade within its own borders, without obstacles put up by provinces. These tariffs and restrictions hinder economic growth. Trade barriers also diminish national unity because, when protectionism is practised, local politics become foremost in citizens' minds. Citizens eventually identify themselves more with the region or province in which they reside than with the country. As prime minister, I would be forceful and persistent in negotiating the removal of interprovincial trade barriers and would enact legislation to do so where necessary.

The few key priorities of federal government I discussed earlier can all be related to standard of living. Often when the term standard of living is used our focus is strictly on financial matters. However, quality of life also encompasses environmental, physical, and social realms. Therefore, I would like to have the federal government focus on our environment, health, and youth.

Environmental regulation and protection should be given redoubled emphasis by the federal government. We must be able to protect our natural wonders and economic resources for the future. Federal and not provincial governments should determine environmental policy, and strict standards must be upheld. Issues such as the disposal of hazardous waste at treatment facilities such as the Swan Hills plant in Alberta would be co-ordinated by the federal government. Waste from neighbouring provinces would be allowed to be disposed of at such plants, and where necessary in other regions new plants would be constructed.

Although education and health are provincial responsibilities, federal transfers in these areas should be maintained and be absolute budgetary priorities. The physical aspect of standard of living and health is fundamental to Canadians' enjoyment of life. Universal medicare should continue to be supplied and enforced. All citizens of this country must be equal in the eyes of the health care system. Canadians believe universal health care is a defining principle of Canadian culture. As prime minister, I would recommit the federal government to this principle. The trend to have individual provinces each radically redefine their delivery of health care and de-insure services must be co-ordinated to prevent the balkanization of health care services. National health standards need to be spelled out, which is something the Canada Health Act does not do. I would direct the Minister of Health to do just that. Provinces would be informed that they must ensure the adequate provision of all services included in the health standards via their public systems.

At the same time, preventative health care should be emphasized. Physical fitness must be stressed. As prime minister, I would be public about my physical fitness regimen and encourage others to do likewise. I would also reinstate fitness awards in schools and workplaces so that we could make fitness a priority for the nation. To discourage unhealthy activity, I would restore federal "sin taxes" on cigarettes to previous levels. Smuggling of these products, if this remains a problem, would then be actively prosecuted by federal authorities instead of being ignored.

While health care would be a priority under my leadership, the system of unemployment insurance would have to be revamped and downsized. Unemployment insurance has become a way of life for too many and allows individuals and groups to adopt the attitude of victimization. Benefit periods and eligibility requirements need to be restricted and chronic recipients forced to move or retrain. Policies where special consideration is given to specific regions of the country under this program would no longer be acceptable. We must not artificially prop up regions and economies that are no longer viable. As a nation we have to accept that, from time to time, economic forces will be such that people will have to uproot, and we should not interfere with this by paying individuals to remain in economically depressed regions.

Looking to Canada's future, it is generally accepted that our youth today are in trouble. Many children are suffering or are not being adequately nurtured. I would use the prime ministership to advocate for children. Band-aid solutions are not the answer. School lunch programs in inner cities, for example, address the pressing problem of hunger; however, they do not tackle the underlying difficulty, which is lack of parental provision or care. As prime minister I would initiate a national program of parenting skills for all new parents and re-establish a commitment to the family as the core unit of our society. In the long run, children who have been properly nurtured and nourished are more productive, less likely to be in trouble or break laws, and can contribute to a safer and better society.

I would propose that high school graduates on a volunteer basis could enrol in a service corps that would work to preserve the nation's environment. Their energy and labour could be harnessed to supplement efforts to maintain and preserve both natural habitats and urban river valleys and parks. Salaries would be minimal, but all living expenses and needs would be provided for in return for an honest commitment. Public relations surrounding this corps would serve to educate others about proper interaction with our environment. The corps would allow youth who had not yet chosen an education or career path to see Canada, while allowing them time to reflect on their upcoming life choices.

In my opinion, Canada's national leaders have been too committed to entrenched practices and slow to accept new patterns of thought. We need to fundamentally restructure, and as the prime minister of Canada I would use the above proposals as the opening phase of transformation. With time and my leadership, Canada would attain loftier heights of unity and prosperity.

TWO

A VISION OF NATIONAL UNITY AND IMPROVED LIVING STANDARDS IN CANADA

• • • • • • • • • •
TREVOR P. B. M. MOAT

Trevor is completing his master's degree in the Department of Systems and Computer Engineering at Carleton University in Ottawa. His thesis will explore new adaptive Digital Signal Processing (DSP) algorithms for conference telephony. He is a former Municipal Ratepayers' representative and a volunteer tutor for adults learning basic skills in mathematics. Trevor has lived in many different regions of the country and, together with his wife, Cecile, has produced approximately forty musical concerts and recitals since 1988, featuring musicians from across Canada. His hobbies include organic gardening and the study of fractal geometry.

THIS PAPER PRESENTS A VISION OF CANADIAN UNITY, AND a road map to improved and equitable living standards for all Canada's citizens. It emanates from the author's fourteen years of work and study in four geographical regions of Canada, and it is written entirely in the hope of improving the lot of all Canadians through unity, tolerance, and long-term planning in business, politics, and social policy. Issues of unity are considered first, since unity is the sole foundation upon which the structural elements of elevated living standards can be built. I invite you to consider what the character of Canada would be if I were its prime minister.

Unifying the Country

No people, nor group of peoples, are "unified" unless their similarities are more evident than their differences. The fruits of our common Canadian heritage have been obscured and starved in the past by the pervasive weeds of misrepresentation and greed, the seeds of which have been cast repeatedly by government at all levels, collectively absent of long-term objectives. Meech, Charlottetown, and the 1982 patriation of the constitution have proven unification cannot be legislated. Governments must create and foster a political environment in which the people themselves assume responsibility for Canada's well-being and provide the direction and impetus necessary to effect positive change.

The adversarial nature of government is largely to blame for the collective angst of Canadian citizens, since it encourages debate only across regional, ethnic, or partisan boundaries. Hence, political discontent has been inadvertently misdirected towards other Canadians. Yet the leaders we elect to unite and guide us are the very embodiment of our distrust. What future has a nation with no faith in its leaders, or the institutions they occupy? Our cynicism will subside only when the opportunities for it to prosper are eliminated. Responsible guidelines for elected and appointed officials must be implemented immediately to ensure they are immune to double-dipping, pork-barrelling, and patronage, the trademarks of present-day partisan politics. A key partnership with private enterprise should be forged to oversee this change.

We should start by rewriting the rules by which our officials are elected. Presently, the sole motivation for political parties is their will to be elected. In many ways, a government's work is done the day it takes office. Worse, it remains largely unaccountable for its actions until forced by law once again to go to the people. Our elections often return an unfair balance of power: overwhelming majorities were won recently in Quebec, Ontario, and Ottawa with less than half of the popular vote; a recent New Brunswick election left over 40 percent of the population unrepresented when all seats were won by a single party. Such elections offer stunted democracy at best, a benign form of short-term totalitarianism in which the majority feel cheated. Rebellion being their only recourse, the disenchanted inadvertently crown subsequent majority governments of very different stripes, thwarting any opportunity for long-term planning and setting the stage for the familiar government charade of "promise, recant, repeal, enact."

When the political pendulum swings violently from right to left and back, catastrophe invariably results. The only sensible means to regain control is to increase the frequency of elections and the accountability of those elected. In so doing, we harmonize the motives of the elected with the electorate, promote social stability, and encourage greater participation in the electoral process. The objective is to enact legislation that forces the transition between successive governments to be as gradual as possible. Here is a blueprint for such legislation.

Canadians would be entitled to elect four governments: municipal, provincial, Commons, and Senate. All ridings in Canada would be assigned to one of four groups, A through D, each of similar size and regional representation. In a given year, each group elects members from their ridings to a different government body, ensuring three-quarters of the seats in each would be unaffected by the election. The next year, the bodies to which each group elects members is shifted by one, such that after four years each group has voted once for each level of government. The strategy is summarized in the table below.

TABLE 1:

Four-Year Unified Election Strategy

Electoral Group	Year One	Year Two	Year Three	Year Four
A	Senate	Municipal	Commons	Provincial
B	Provincial	Senate	Municipal	Commons
C	Commons	Provincial	Senate	Municipal
D	Municipal	Commons	Provincial	Senate

One might argue that the resulting governments would be held hostage by frequent elections. Indeed, minority victories and frequent elections do handcuff governments to a certain extent under our present system. However, there is no greater likelihood that minority governments would ensue under this revamped structure, since "good" governments would be rewarded annually with renewed support. At every level, this system allows the electorate to support or snub parties in power on a regular basis by electing or rejecting their allies in other governing bodies or in subsequent years. It ensures regular voter–member feedback and prevents destructive policy shifts after elections. Furthermore, it invites the establishment of a single, national electoral system to administer each level of government in every riding. This would replace the heavily redundant electoral systems we presently employ.

Such changes may seem radical, but they are the reality under which free enterprise operates every day. Corporations spend millions annually surveying their markets, soliciting customer feedback, and crafting plans to make their shares and wares more attractive to investors and consumers. Indeed, they have no choice; they cannot survive without ongoing support from their "electorate." In this way, business provides a very good model for government. The trouble is, government and business hold mutual distrust for one another, justifiably perhaps, because their objectives are inherently different: government is motivated once every five years by elections; business is motivated daily by profit.

Clearly, a new spirit of co-operation is in order. Business is the economic engine of society. However, government and business also bear joint responsibility for social welfare, since so many business assets (skilled labour, infrastructure, public investment, and the like) descend directly from government-funded programs. There are two key components of corporate social duty: first, businesses must help implement and maintain a revised corporate taxation strategy that reduces waste and eliminates frivolous deductions; second, they must take a pro-active role in the training and education of their most valuable asset — their people.

Corporate tax law requires numerous philosophical changes. Earnings reinvested should be subject to reduced tax rates; earnings that are not — such as those paid out in salaries, bonuses, allowances, and the like — should be taxed at higher rates. Tax credits for all entertainment expenses, and for losses sustained through poor investment practices, should be eliminated immediately. Deductions for autos should be limited to $20,000 undepreciated cost. Research tax credits should be available only to small firms developing new technologies, not to wealthy monoliths recycling old ones. Furthermore, tax-collection procedures should be updated. Small businesses should file returns annually, not quarterly, saving millions in unproductive accounting fees and lost time.

In return, governments must facilitate growth of new enterprises and technologies to ensure corporate and national survival in the global marketplace. Key responsibilities include the development of modern infrastructure and environmental policy, provision of venture capital incentives and entrepreneurial support services, creation of a climate for international trade, and the redistribution of wealth through fair and simple taxation. Infrastructure and tax reform are the two areas that require immediate attention.

Twenty-first-century infrastructure will consist of fibre-optic networks, efficient mass-transit systems, and premier educational institutions. Presently, few initiatives from any level of government are forthcoming to lay their foundations. To ignore them is fiscal suicide in the long term, because advanced technology and education are Canada's greatest comparative advantages. Immediate co-operation across all levels of government is required to design our future infrastructure.

The government should streamline its commitment to environmental protection through legislation targeting end-use products rather than manufacturers. For example, to enact a law that all newsprint produced in Canada must have 50 percent recycled content would amount to a boon for foreign suppliers. However, legislation banning the sale of newspapers with less than 50 percent post-consumer content would engender immediate interest from entrepreneurial suppliers, whether or not they have an environmental conscience. Manufacturing taxes for non-recyclable and environmentally insensitive products and packaging should be levied at source. Corporate tax incentives and pro-active environmental laws can be applied to benefit many facets of business and society. Being experts in innovation and efficiency, business should be called upon to provide proposals to make these improvements.

The tax system, the lifeblood of our social structure, presents the most rewarding challenge imaginable to any finance minister. The following principles should be introduced as quickly as possible.

- *Wealth should be recycled within Canada.* Foreign ownership of Canadian debt should be tapered off by phasing in an external-ownership tax on government bonds. Offshore tax shelters must be dismantled, since they discriminate against the poor.
- *Short-term investment should be discouraged.* Realized capital gains (including those from designated principal residences) should be taxed 100 percent in the first three months after purchase, the rate declining by 10 percent for each quarter year of ownership thereafter. This tax would discourage "flipping," which drove housing

markets in Toronto and Vancouver well beyond the reach of most citizens. Long-term investment strengthens and stabilizes our markets, currency, and housing. Speculators suck the blood out of them.

- *RRSPs should provide retirement comfort for all, not wealth for a few.* Contributions to registered retirement savings plan accounts worth more than twenty-five times the average Canadian's annual income should be disallowed. The first $2,000 of annual contribution should receive much more favourable tax treatment than the remainder. A declining benefit would encourage all taxpayers to contribute annually enough to house and feed themselves in retirement, while providing lesser subsidies thereafter to those who can afford them.

- Finally, GST should be applied to all brokerage fees, since brokers' services consist of buying and selling goods. Foreign investments should be taxed lightly, since such taxes discourage investment and therefore deprive Canadian corporations of much-needed capital. Lottery winnings over $1,000 should be subject to a flat 10 percent tax. This would not be sufficient to deter those who view lotteries as a viable means of wealth generation from participating in them.

Each of these small tugs on the broad belt of taxation offers the benefit of being purely progressive: they target only those who can, and should, afford them. Better living standards are bound to follow, since increased social funding would be available.

Improving Living Standards

A nation's standard of living should be regarded as that afforded its least fortunate citizens. With this in mind, Canada provides living standards for some comparable to those of Third World nations. This disenfranchisement is a sure sign of an unhappy society. Mexico, for example, produced more millionaires per capita in 1994 than any other nation, yet in the same year its people suffered under immense political and financial turbulence. Americans have also endured unparalleled racial and socio-political tension recently, and a vast devaluation in their greenback. Japan and Singapore, on the other hand, benefit from very high literacy, good health, very low unemployment and crime, and a solid currency. The greater the disparity between rich and poor, the lower the standard of living.

Granted, throwing money at poverty merely thwarts initiative; one must maintain motivation and dignity to thrive. Education engenders these attributes in the majority of people. Having said this, there is more to an education than what can be taught in the classroom. In a land as diverse as Canada, individual cultural awareness is crucial to prevent undue influence from opportunistic politicians and journalists. Mandatory cultural exchanges, divided deliberately across ethnic, geographical, linguistic, and/or socio-economic boundaries, should be implemented to ensure all public school students develop an understanding of their remarkable national heritage. Furthermore, our flagship social programs — education and medicare — require changes to make their delivery better and more efficient.

Certain tools of modern society are taught improperly, if at all, in our public schools. Basic courses in personal financial planning and business principles should be readily available, if not mandatory, in secondary schools. Private-sector professionals — financial planners, engineers, bankers, brokers — should direct these courses on a rotating basis. Such programs would lend practical applications to existing math and science skills, as well as encourage student participation in business activities and business investment in our social infrastructure.

From a young age, students must develop self-discipline and goal-setting skills. So often they accept, by default, that their courses require passing grades, not excellence. Here is where the private-sector model can be employed most effectively. Business today cannot survive merely by setting mediocre goals and achieving them — a goal that is readily achievable is scarcely worth setting. A child's education should consist of a series of personal, well-defined, and manageable goals interwoven with strong threads of encouragement of self-learning and exploration from parents, teachers, and mentors. Motivation is the key to success for children, students, and corporations alike.

To foster personal motivation in post-secondary students, government should reduce direct subsidies to colleges and universities. Instead, students should assume much greater personal responsibility for their education by funding it themselves through an expanded student loans program. Grants and preferred repayment schedules would be offered based on the usefulness of one's degree to society, one's willingness to remain in Canada after graduation, and, of course, the grades achieved.

Repayment plans should be as accommodating as possible. Income tax refunds should be withheld in the event of default.

Two major adjustments to medicare should be made: first, its focus must be shifted towards prevention rather than treatment; second, its mandate should migrate gradually from that of a single-fee system towards one of obligatory public medical insurance, with fees escalating according to personal lifestyle.

Complementary medicines — naturopathic, homeopathic, and chiropractic, among others — should be regulated and fully sanctioned by the medical system, since they represent personal, long-term investment in self-management of health care and illness prevention. Universality, in providing equal treatment for all, discriminates against users who practise preventative medicine. Some people invite illness through negligence — be it chronic (smoking, for example) or incidental (failure to wear seatbelts) — and higher premiums should apply for services to treat the consequences. Our right to subsidized health care should not exceed our personal responsibility to care for ourselves.

Conclusion

Our dedication to Canada as the land of our ancestors, or as a new land free of persecution, represents our greatest hope for unity. While some issues concerning business, politics, and social programming are addressed herein, the key is to recognize the need for consistent, long-term planning in these fields. If I were the prime minister of Canada, I would do everything in my power to make certain that governments, executives, and citizens alike accept joint responsibility for maintaining social programs and national unity.

I am grateful for the invitation to share my long-held sentiments for Canada. It is my hope that they will be heard by those of equal conviction who can help effect change for the better.

THREE

SOLUTIONS, NOT SILENCE

• • • • • • • • • •
AMY MACFARLANE

A native of Summerside, Prince Edward Island, Amy recently graduated from Acadia University with a Bachelor of Arts degree in economics and business and is currently completing a Bachelor of Business Administration degree. In 1995, Amy was awarded the Governor General's Medal for achieving the highest academic standing among graduating students. She also received an award for her outstanding involvement in, leadership of, and contribution to Acadia University. On campus, she was a volunteer for the SMILE program, which assists mentally and physically challenged children. She was captain of the Acadia women's rugby team and a former PEI Junior Female Athlete of the Year who competed in the 1987 and 1991 Canada Winter Games.

CANADA IS A LAND OF WEALTH AND OPPORTUNITY. IT IS A land of promise and potential. Why, then, is Canada a land filled with problems? In recent years, the trend in Canadian politics has been towards a weakened family unit, state dependency, and uncontrolled government spending. Cynicism regarding the political process and cultural tensions have been growing. In short, these are the problems. I believe there exists a silent majority of Canadians who want this trend reversed, who want to see a return to responsible, commonsense governing. Unfortunately, distrust and disillusionment with their own government have ensured their silence. However, solutions, not silence, are our hope for the future.

Preventing the improvement of Canada's standard of living are two main problems: our nation's debt and our high levels of unemployment.

Both issues must be addressed before any improvement can occur. Obviously, then, the best way to improve our living standards in the long run is to accept a decline in the short run while we tackle these two problems wholeheartedly. Then we can turn to new efforts to unify our country.

Strengthening the Family Unit

To address the nation's debt, we must first focus on strengthening the family unit. We "must publicly recognize the family once and for all as our primary transmitter of values from generation to generation; our most basic tool of wealth creation."[1] It is from our families that we learn the importance of freedom, responsibility, self-reliance, hard work, and perseverance — all values inherent in our Canadian culture. Government policy must encourage a strengthened family unit, yet such is not the case in Canada today. For instance, a prominent Canadian, Tom Kent, writes in his book *Getting Ready for 1999*: "the full cost of child-care should be reimbursed for the single parent in employment or training."[2] Attitudes such as this threaten to destroy our traditional family unit. Why would any parent legally marry when remaining single (if only on paper) would guarantee full government funding for child care? Certainly, a "live-in" relationship would make more economic sense. Canada's movement towards universal day-care is dangerous, to say the least.

Income tax legislation

Canada's income tax laws presently do little to encourage a strong family unit. Under our current system, tax laws dramatically favour a family with two working parents each earning $40,000 annually as compared with one working parent earning $80,000 annually. By taxing the family unit, as opposed to the individual, this inequality could easily be solved. Fairness must mean that people with the same resources pay the same taxes. Although a detailed restructuring of our income tax laws is not possible in this proposal, it is sufficient to note that efforts must also be made to tighten loopholes to ensure families are taxed based on all types of income.

To strengthen the family unit, the Canadian government must boldly move beyond these improvements. One possibility is an attractive tax incentive for families with one stay-at-home parent. If, after factoring in child care costs and a tax reduction, the incremental benefit of a second income is no longer appealing, the trend towards two working parents will reverse itself.

A tax incentive for the family with a stay-at-home parent would also help address our unemployment issue. Currently, the labour supply in Canada exceeds the labour demand. Eliminating the appeal of two working parents would greatly reduce the size of our workforce.

Responsibility of the Individual and Family

With a strengthened family unit, responsibility for one's well-being can gradually shift away from the government and back into the hands of the individual and the family. Too many Canadians are dependent on the state, viewing social programs as their right instead of the privilege that they are. To improve Canada's standard of living, we must shift from state dependency to self-reliance because, simply put, we cannot maintain our current levels of social spending. Government in Canada is too large. "By June, 1992, Canada had a ratio of one government employee for every 5.5 citizens and was one of the highest taxed jurisdictions in the world."[3] Deficit reduction must take the form of reduced spending, since tax increases will only result in more skilful tax evasion and less incentive to increase one's earnings. Without a doubt, this must involve a massive restructuring of our social programs.

Unemployment insurance legislation

Reform of our unemployment insurance legislation is a must. "In 1992, over 54% of all households in Canada receiving UIC earned over $53,000 annually."[4] In my home province of Prince Edward Island, exploitation of unemployment insurance has become a way of life. Many fishermen, for instance, earn more during the fishing seasons than other Islanders earn in an entire year; then they comfortably relax with their sizeable UI cheques during the off-season. I chose this profession as an example only; it is by no means the only industry that skilfully distorts the true purpose of unemployment insurance by using it as a supplement to seasonal earnings. Worse yet, our government make-work projects are designed specifically to give recipients their "ten stamps" necessary to collect unemployment insurance, allowing their dependence on the state to proliferate. Not exactly leading by example.

Unemployment insurance must return to its original purpose — to protect workers against temporary and unforeseen job loss. Like any private-sector insurance program, UI benefits must be financed solely by contributions. Eligibility must be tightened and the number of weeks of contribution increased. In addition, our UI program presently subsidizes people for remaining in unproductive regions of the country. Incentives must be built into the system to ensure people are redistributed to new sources of wealth in other regions of Canada.

Welfare

In an attempt to eliminate poverty, Canada has deteriorated into a welfare state. Government justifies the huge amount of money spent on social programs since it redistributes resources from the wealthy to the poor. Yet, "if you exclude the six billion dollars that government contributes to welfare, 76% of social spending will go to middle and higher income Canadians."[5] Statistically, the normal distribution will prevent government from achieving equal outcomes for all. Instead, the government should focus on providing equal *opportunities* for all. "The role — one government has vastly exceeded today — is like that of a referee who regulates and adjudicates a game but does not play it. Rather, he creates a just and fair environment in which the rules are established equally for all players, who can play as hard or as lazily as they wish."[6]

The notion of universality, in terms of social programs, is both inefficient and unsustainable. Canada must define the "truly needy" — those without basic food, clothing, and shelter. It is for the "truly needy" that welfare is intended. Having said this, welfare still robs people of incentive. Requiring able welfare recipients to work would change this while providing recipients with work experience. Though this idea may sound radical, a November 30, 1989, Gallup Poll reports that "84% of Canadians surveyed think welfare recipients should be made to work."[7] In addition, welfare must be viewed as a last resort, forcing Canadians to rely first on themselves and then on their families.

Medicare

A final area in need of massive restructuring is medicare. With no restraints on the provision of medical services, demand will always

exceed supply. "Socialized medicine must inevitably lead to deterioration of quality and availability."[8] Just ask a family member of a Canadian who died while on the waiting list for heart surgery at a Canadian
hospital. Canada is the only Western nation where the provision of
private medical services is illegal. Preventing Canadians from purchasing the most essential and sacred service of all is criminal. Canada
must dismantle its medicare system. Instead, medical and catastrophic
insurance should be compulsory for all Canadians. However, any
attempt to reform medicare is subject to irrational appeals to Canadians' emotions. For instance, Tom Kent writes, "for access to healthcare
to depend on ability to pay, or for a child on the parents' ability to pay,
is entirely unacceptable in a democratic society."[9] But dismantling
medicare would not mean this. Canadians unable to afford private
medical insurance, the "truly needy," would be provided for by the
state. As it stands, Canada cannot afford medicare, and as our financial
position worsens, so too will our ability to provide essential medical
services.

Unifying the Country
Addressing both our national debt and our high levels of unemployment
will have a unifying effect on Canada. However, the underlying sources
of disunity will remain. "Many have lamented the absence of strong
national feeling, of shared values, and abiding commitment but few have
attempted to correct the underlying structural and institutional failures
that account for the situation."[10] Here, I will attempt to do just that.

One underlying cause of disunity in Canada is our lack of faith in
the political process. The following recommendations focus on restoring credibility in our political system.

Electoral reform
Presently in Canada, our electoral system is based on plurality, a method
of election whereby the candidate with the largest number of votes
wins. This method tends to create government majorities where none are
created by the voters. Also, plurality refuses representation to minority
parties, who, despite winning consistent support nationwide, cannot
concentrate enough support in a single constituency to gain representation. This under-representation of minorities has resulted in violence,

illustrated by the Oka crisis, and alienation, exemplified by Quebec, driven to separation as an extreme.

The electoral system in Canada should be based on proportional representation, a method that follows from the principle that "a democratic legislature should be representative of all the interests and viewpoints of the electorate."[11] Under proportional representation, seats are allocated in proportion to the total popular votes received. A party receiving 10 percent of the total vote, for example, would be awarded 10 percent of the seats in government. Such a system would accommodate the modern-day reality of a multicultural Canada.

Senate reform is imperative if faith in our political process is to be restored. To garner legitimacy in the eyes of the public, senators must be elected. Patronage appointments by outgoing prime ministers only foster Canadians' growing cynicism. Allocating Senate seats more equitably among regions would enable the Senate to become a forum for regional representation where senators, freed of party discipline, could actively voice the concerns of their constituents.

Accountability

In Canada, we have few checks and balances on political power. Nothing demonstrates this more than the current financial fiasco we find ourselves in. Fiscally, governments must be held accountable. Contributions for unemployment insurance or pension plans should be earmarked specifically for these programs, not tossed into general tax revenue. As mentioned earlier, benefits for such programs should be financed solely through employee contributions. Government departments, at all levels, must be required to balance their books. Constitutional limits on spending, as proposed by Milton Friedman, are not an extreme but rather a necessity.

Changes, such as those outlined above, are inevitable if we hope to replace cynicism with credibility in our political system.

The Quebec question

Another underlying cause of disunity in Canada is our relationship with the province of Quebec. Obviously, the future of Canada depends on "a degree of willingness on the part of its members to tolerate the continuance of the association."[12] A new equilibrium in Canada can be established only by conceding autonomy in cultural matters to the provinces. Each province will determine its *own* language policy. Of course, what this means is an end to official bilingualism in Canada. "Linguistic duality is a vision of Canada at variance with the social reality most English-speaking Canadians experience. Most anglophones have little or no contact with francophones."[13] Furthermore, when I travel to Quebec or any francophone community, I expect to be immersed in the French culture — most definitely, I do not expect services in English. Nationwide official bilingualism does not reflect the reality of Canada's composition. In British Columbia, for instance, it would be far more useful to know Chinese as a second language than French. In fact, "one quarter of Canada's population belongs to ethnic groups other than the 'charter' British and French majority."[14]

Understanding our history

"What a nation remembers about itself, its history, is a major source of its political culture."[15] Until we understand our history, we will not understand our politics, and until then, we will remain a nation divided. A commission on Canadian studies "recommended that no student be allowed to graduate from high school or university without 'certain minimum levels of knowledge' about the political institutions and political cultures of their country."[16] This is one recommendation that should never have been shelved. To work towards a unified nation and secure Canada's future, we need an educated electorate. To know where we are going, we have to know where we have been.

Creating an emotional bond

So far, I have proposed rational solutions to unify the country, but I have ignored an entire portion of our thinking — the emotional side. The future of Canada depends on establishing common interests. Perhaps this means reaffirming our belief in freedom, self-reliance, or the family. Or, possibly, it involves focusing our energies towards a common goal, such as reducing unemployment. One only has to look at the successful Participaction or anti-smoking campaigns to know attitudes can be changed. Apathy towards our political system can be changed to activism. Indifference can be changed to involvement. If Canada is to remain united, our love for our country, our desire to be Canadians, must supersede our cultural and regional differences.

Perhaps there are other Canadians who agree with some or all of the ideas discussed here. I hope my ideas will at least foster debate and encourage others to speak out. As mentioned earlier, solutions, not silence, are our hope for the future. If our economy is to improve and if our nation is to remain united, change is needed. Together, we can demand that change. Together, we can ensure Canada remains a land of promise and potential.

Notes

1. William D. Gairdner, *The Trouble with Canada* (Toronto: Stoddart Publishing Co. Ltd., 1994), p. 83.
2. Tom Kent, *Getting Ready for 1999* (Halifax: Institute for Research on Public Policy, 1989), p. 118.
3. Gairdner, p. 14.
4. Gairdner, p. 229.
5. John Raymond, "Burns Fry Economic Outlook," *The Globe and Mail*, August 26, 1988.
6. Gairdner, p. 55.
7. Gairdner, p. 164.
8. Gairdner, p. 305.
9. Kent, p. 101
10. David V. J. Bell, *The Roots of Disunity* (Toronto: Oxford University Press, 1992), p. 191.
11. Arend Lijphart and Bernard Grofman, *Choosing an Electoral System* (New York: Praeger Publishers, 1984), p. 5.
12. David Cameron, *Nationalism, Self-determination and the Quebec Question* (Toronto: Macmillan of Canada, 1974), p. 74.
13. Michael O'Keefe, "An Analysis of Attitudes towards Official Language Policy among Anglophones," Office of the Commission of Official Languages, Policy Analysis Branch, October, 1990, p. 8.
14. Bell, p. 150.
15. Bell, p. 5
16. T. H. B. Simons, "To Know Ourselves: The Report on the Commission on Canadian Studies" (Ottawa: Association of Universities and Colleges of Canada, 1975), p. 126.

FOUR

SMALL IS BEAUTIFUL: HOW COMMUNITY GOVERNMENTS WILL ENHANCE DEMOCRACY AND MAKE CANADA PROSPER

• • • • • • • • • •

BAHRAD A. SOKHANSANJ

*B*ahrad is in his second year in the Department of Engineering Physics at the University of Saskatchewan in his hometown of Regina. He was project group leader at the university's Engineering Fair, "Spectrum 95," where he and seven other team members worked on a model hearing-system project. He was also a member of the university's debating society and a participant in the Model United Nations Club on campus.

CANADA AT THE END OF THE TWENTIETH CENTURY IS IN crisis. A new generation is coming to terms with the realization that they will be the first who will be poorer than their parents. People in their late forties are watching their jobs, white- or blue-collar, disappear. Canadians are affected by all of the stresses bothering people elsewhere: free trade, environmental problems, and a technological revolution that is making thousands of jobs obsolete. Even worse, in the midst of all this social and economic instability, governments across Canada are crippled by the fear that massive debts will cause a fiscal crisis.

Why Canada Must Change

In 1867, William Dawson of McGill University said, of one of the infant Dominion's few national symbols: "[The beaver] is a type of unvarying instincts and old-world traditions. He does not improve and becomes extinct rather than change his ways."[1] Today, Canada is one of the few countries that possesses in abundance the resources required to succeed in the new world order: energy, water, minerals, an educated population, a sustainable birth-rate, democratic and free-enterprise traditions. Left alone, like beavers, Canada's governments might be able to muddle through and barely escape extinction. On the other hand, with the proper changes made in its administrative structure, Canada could thrive and even move beyond its contemporaries. Why merely hope to survive if effective use of Canada's resources can make our nation great?

An Activist Response without Enlarging Government

Political bankruptcy has accompanied fiscal bankruptcy in Canadian capitals. Faced with permanent poverty for 15 percent of Canadians, a collective national debt of over $600 billion, and voter discontent, bureaucrats have run out of creative solutions. This is no excuse for inaction, because Canada needs new political initiatives, now more than ever. But there is still one level of government that is close enough to people to effectively respond to their needs: local government. By giving communities the means to respond to their residents' needs, Canadian governments can continue to play an active role in the advancement of Canadians without increasing the size of the already bloated provincial and federal bureaucracies.

What Communities Are Doing Today

The BNA Act of 1867 placed municipal governments under the jurisdiction of the provinces. Provinces established counties, cities, towns, and rural municipalities. Today, a typical city, like Saskatoon, for example, has these responsibilities: fire-fighting, police, water and sewage, transit, garbage, parks and recreation centres, snow removal, insect control, and maybe an auditorium and arena. To fund such municipal activities, an average family in Saskatoon pays just 1.4 percent of its income in property taxes ($701)[2] to a city with a balanced budget and a triple-A credit rating.

The municipality is only one of the community governments currently in existence. School districts administer primary and secondary education on a local level under the direction of provincial governments. In Saskatchewan, regional health districts will soon administer hospitals and health care services, also under the direction of the provincial government. And there are other community organizations that are not official governments. For example, the United Way collects and distributes around $1.5 million in charitable donations. Communities operate art galleries, auditoriums, and libraries that preserve and enhance culture. Cities and rural municipalities in Saskatchewan and elsewhere administer "community bond" programs that raise money within a community for use in economic development.

Overall, the various community governments have proven more successful at meeting their citizens' needs than federal and provincial governments. Many community administrators remain popular and respected in an age of voter discontent. The exceptions that prove the rule are large cities, where there is a great distance between voter and governor. The only way to get elected in Canada without having a lot of private funding from special interest groups is to run for one of the community governments. More democratic and more efficient, communities are succeeding where federal and provincial governments, with their many resources, are failing.

Why Higher Levels of Government Fail

There are three reasons why Canadian governments are failing to meet their citizens' needs. First, the distance between government and its electorate has severely damaged democracy. People feel, with justification, that a government administering millions of citizens over a massive geographic area cannot respond to their personal needs. Because of the need to run extensive national campaigns, governments respond only to special interests and their campaign contributors. When was the last time you spoke to your MP? When was the last time your MP listened?

The second reason why higher levels of government have failed is the arrogance and elitism that have arisen in the capitals. As social engineers, bureaucrats have shown incredible contempt for the society that they are seeking to repair. Policy has become an end unto itself, rather than a means of effectively responding to the people's real concerns about the environment, poverty, and labour standards. One example of failed policy is the much-vaunted federal Green Plan. While it was produced on beautiful recycled paper, the Green Plan failed even to begin to reconcile the conflict between development and conservation. Filled with promising goals and objectives, the plan lacked any substance and has, in any case, been quietly dropped by the Chrétien government. The Green Plan is a white elephant, representing the worst excesses of bureaucrats gone mad.

The third reason for the failure of higher levels of government is that

Canada is a multicultural, regional nation. Provinces are often required to govern an extraordinarily diverse population. Because of regional differences, government initiatives are never universally acceptable. Gun registration, designed to deal with concerns about growing urban crime, has resulted in angry rural opposition. Bilingualism has placed Ottawa elites against an unlikely coalition of westerners and Quebec nationalists. Agricultural policy cannot reconcile the interests of export-oriented western grain farmers and eastern dairy farmers interested in preserving their domestic markets. Welfare, economic development — the list goes on and on: Canada's governments are incapable of creating effective solutions for Canadians' diverse problems.

Clearly the best solution to Canada's problems is not a top-down approach directed by the federal government, an approach that has been seen to fail; rather, it is a bottom-up approach directed by people at the community level. Communities built Canada, and only communities can make Canada great.

Details of the Decentralization of Authority

The decentralization of authority to community governments will be a gradual process. Pilot projects and public consultation can ensure that the theories outlined in this essay result in concrete improvement in the lives of Canadians. Why go through the inconvenience of dramatically changing Canada's administrative structure if no benefit can be derived from it? Such idiocy should be limited to the activities of bureaucrats.

The first powers to be transferred to community governments will be powers of implementation, similar to a school district's power of implementing provincial education policy at the local level. Economic development, social services (unemployment insurance, welfare, Old Age Security), culture spending, and health care will be administered at the local level on the basis of policy direction from the federal and provincial governments.

I believe that there should be a separate community authority for each different area of policy. Multiple community governments have the best chance for meaningful public participation. In larger cities, there may be multiple administrative districts within the same community, again enhancing public participation. Part of community government is decreasing the distance between citizens and their administrators.

The Continuing Role of Higher Levels of Government

Even in those responsibilities decentralized to communities, federal and provincial governments will continue to exert influence. Higher levels of government will set the principles that communities will implement in their administrations. The division of responsibility will be similar to that in education: the federal government is responsible for national funding and broad standards, provincial governments are responsible for curriculum and regulations, and school boards administer actual schools within their districts. The continuing role of provincial and federal governments will ensure that programs remain adequate in all regions of the country. Computer technology and modern communications will allow people to move easily from community to community without losing services, adapting community government to today's highly mobile society.

The federal government will be left to do what it does best: draft broad policy designed to improve the common good. The federal government might apply a social charter that would have the same influence in social services, labour rights, and environmental regulation that the Charter of Rights and Freedoms has had in the application of laws. The federal government will be free to concentrate on improving Canada's international economic and political standing.

Gradual Progress: The Future of Communities

Gradually, community governments will gain more and more power over the initiation and development of public policy. Aspects of the Criminal Code might be left up to communities to decide. For example, Metro Toronto's council recently asked the federal government to legalize prostitution and let cities try to regulate it. Eventually, issues like prostitution, gambling, gun control, and business regulation will be considered at the community level (while still subject to national principles). Communities will form coalitions based around common interests and start assuming greater responsibility. Provinces might slowly disappear as political talent follows political clout to the community level. Communities, using modern technology to facilitate inexpensive and efficient public consultations, will become organs of direct democracy. Community governments will enhance democracy, consult citizens more often, and increase public confidence in government.

Funding Community Governments

The community governments will collect taxes and fees, much as school boards and city councils do today. They will also receive funding from provincial and federal income and sales taxes; however, taxing responsibilities will gradually shift to the community level. Higher levels of government can use their financial influence to make sure that community governments are maintaining fundamental principles of service. Community authorities will be expected to balance their budgets, ensuring fiscal discipline. In case of economic disaster, an Emergency Community Transfer Fund (ECTF) will dispense funds to communities in economic trouble (rural communities in drought, industrial areas in recession, fishing communities during the cod moratorium, etc.). When a community has a surplus it will pay into the ECTF, and then draw funds from it if a recession causes a deficit. Like the crop insurance program it is similar to, the ECTF will ensure financial stability in all regions of Canada.

How Community Governments Will Reduce the Deficit

Community governments are uncomfortably close to angry taxpayers, limited in their means of carrying a debt, and generally efficient. Communities will spend less money than the federal government. The savings to the national budget will be in these areas: social programs (38 percent of federal spending), fiscal arrangements like shared-cost programs and transfer payments (12 percent), industrial support (2.5 percent), and heritage/communications (1.8 percent).[3] The efficiency of community governments, along with the elimination of costly bureaucracies and federal-provincial duplication, will save billions of dollars. Some have suggested that government waste and federal-provincial duplication account for as much as 30 percent of federal spending in these areas.

Even a minimum saving of 10 percent at just the federal level would result in considerable gains. In 1994–95, the government projected spending at approximately $161.9 billion[4] and a deficit of $40.5 billion. Thus, a mere 10 percent cut in the areas affected by community governments would result in a 5.5 percent cut in government expenditures ($8.9 billion) and a 22 percent cut in the deficit *without affecting the nature of programs* (although the method of delivering programs would change). Of course, this is just a starting point. Depending on the efficiency of communities in managing their affairs, cuts of 15 to 25 percent in federal spending could occur. Community governments will allow governments to remain activist and cut the deficit at the same time.

Quebec in an Era of Community Governments

In today's Canada, Quebec's concerns about the security of its culture and language have threatened national unity. Quebec might well perceive that community governments will stop the province from acting to preserve its culture. If the communities within Quebec wanted, the province could retain greater authority over culture and economic development than envisioned in my plan. Quebec could retain the power to act in the collective interests of its people while still allowing communities greater autonomy in social services and health care.

Meanwhile, in Canada as a whole, petty rivalries and jealousies will cease. Relations between communities will become paramount. Experience shows that people acting at the community level in Quebec and the rest of Canada understand each other much better than provincial politicians, with their flaming rhetoric and grandstanding.

A New Canadian Patriotism

Shortly after Confederation, a prominent Canadian politician, Edward Blake, said, "The future of Canada depends very largely upon the cultivation of a national spirit. We must find some common ground on which to unite, some common aspiration to be shared, and I think it can be found alone in the cultivation of that national spirit to which I have referred."[5]

For 128 years, Canadian artists, politicians, and academics have searched for Canada's elusive national spirit. The artists, politicians, and academics do not realize that Canadians have *already forged* their national spirit. Canadians are pioneers trying to survive in a harsh environment. Canada's national spirit is the spirit of immigrants from all over the world trying to build lives in one of the world's harshest habitable areas. Canadians formed communities to work together and improve their lives.

Community government is not a blind step forward. Rather, it is a return to the community-based way of solving problems that existed in Canada before governments started to manage people's lives. With community governments, Canadians will once again rely on each other, and communities will continue to build Canada. A new patriotism will arise in Canada: the national spirit of communities co-operating to achieve the collective good of all Canadians.

Community Governments: An Activist Solution

Community governments represent an activist solution to Canada's problems. Because their solutions are more efficient and more appropriate to local concerns, community governments will increase democracy, make public participation easier, decrease the deficit, and improve government service. Community governments will allow activist politics to continue without contributing to the deficit or increasing the size of government.

If I were elected prime minister, I would be elected on a promise to institute community government. I would use my political clout, as well as the financial clout of transfer payments, to convince provinces to join me in transferring responsibility to communities. At first, community governments would be gradually established, perhaps beginning with aboriginal communities. However, as community governments began to prove their success, the process of decentralization would be accelerated. My government would thus be free to spend its time and energies ensuring the common good of the nation.

Canada in the twenty-first century, free of regional rivalries, will be able to achieve its destiny of greatness. Communities are the strength of this nation; let us use that muscle to move forward.

Notes

1. This anecdote is from Desmond Morton's *A Short History of Canada* (Edmonton: Hurtig Publishers Ltd., 1983), p. 15.
2. Source: City of Saskatoon.
3. All financial data for 1994–95 come from *How Ottawa Spends 1994–95: Making Change*, ed. Susan D. Phillips (Ottawa: Carleton University Press, 1994), appendix.
4. The 1995–96 budget calls for reducing spending such that the deficit is reduced to $24 billion. For consistency, I will use 1994–95 figures.

5. This quote, attributed to Edward Blake, is from Pierre Trudeau's *Pierre Trudeau Speaks Out on Meech Lake*, ed. Donald Johnston (Toronto: General Paperbacks, 1990), p. 23.

FIVE

SAFE AT HOME

• • • • • • • • • •
CHRISTOPHER A. JONES

A resident of Millbrook, Ontario, Chris is completing his last year at Bishop's University, where he is pursuing a degree in Political Studies while also studying Urban Geography and History. After a brief stint as a disc jockey last year, Chris became station manager for CJMQ, a campus radio station serving the local community. Chris also wrote for the campus newspaper and was a member of the United Nations Club.

FEW PASSIONS FUEL AS FIERCE A DEVOTION AND HAVE more in common than politics and baseball. For the highly skilled, the practice of each has evolved into a fine art. Both feature intense individual competition, though success can be achieved only as part of a team. And, like baseball, politics is designed to break your heart.

Not so much the art of the possible, as it is often described, politics is rather an imperfect means to solve complex problems with the most limited of tools. To accomplish anything of virtue is very nearly impossible. To do this, however, to aspire to lofty heights in a realm fraught with limitations, is among the most principled and meritorious of human endeavours. In the words of Vaclav Havel, former president of Czechoslovakia: "There is only one thing I will not concede: that it might be meaningless to strive in a good cause." In the words of Jackie Robinson, the legendary Brooklyn Dodger: "A life is not important except in the impact it has on other lives." To fight the good fight, to overcome apparently insurmountable obstacles and achieve something near perfection in a less than perfect world, is the ultimate human end. Through politics, certain individuals are given the opportunity, and are entrusted with the power, to move society that much closer to this distant perfection.

If I were thrust into such a position, my tenure would be marked by three ever-present principles: localism, equality, and environment. To guide this nation towards a tomorrow of unity and prosperity is a monumental task, far beyond the reach of any one person. With these fundamentals close to heart, however, and in taking the first steps so that others may follow — giving the hands of all Canadians a chance to touch upon this process — one person may have a tremendous impact and achieve what was once thought to be impossible.

Today, it is apparent that many Canadians feel not only alienated from government but also openly hostile towards it. This widening gap between a nation's citizens and a nation's leaders, if allowed to continue, will entail grave consequences for this country. Such a rift is what toppled Rome, and, in this age of separatism and anger, frustration and hopelessness, Canada may inevitably follow. There is a remedy for this sickness, however, in the form of determined *localism* and a new search for community.

At a ball game, it is far easier to get a sense of the action from the dugout than from the upper deck of a monolithic stadium. For citizens reduced to the role of anonymous spectators, government has evolved into something impersonal and suffocating, regarded as an omnipresent force capable of inflicting significant harm, with little evident capacity for contributing to the greater good. Politics has become the realm of the elite and the privileged, a place where ordinary individuals have become lost in the shuffle, and where, for most, faith and trust are relics of the past. This is not a climate that fosters unity.

Government must become something else, a product of all our creative energies, something that can be felt, affected, and believed. It must be brought closer to the people of Canada. It must be capable of meeting the distinct needs of substantially different places, tailored to each particular situation. Thus, localism is a necessary path.

Municipal government is very often powerless, though it is in the best position to positively effect change. And municipal government is the most accessible of jurisdictions, though it often attracts the least electoral participation. When those who pull the strings are far away, in terms of both physical and psychological distance, a sense of unity and trust is not inspired. But when those in power walk side by side with citizens on the street, only a handshake away, a sense of purpose and community will result.

A new system of localities must be created, with their boundaries based upon existing electoral districts, each home to about 100,000 Canadians. A patchwork quilt of hundreds of constituencies is not a complete answer, however. These distinct regions must be strung together by a strong federal government, providing the ties that bind them into a cohesive whole. Through the federal government's continued exercise of defence, financial, and foreign relation roles, to name but a few, and bolstered by such institutions as the CBC, Canada Post, and other national crown corporations, this ideal could be attained. But this vision, a collection of local governments held together by an overarching federal government, can be achieved only through dramatic restructuring, at the expense of a particular level of administration: the provinces.

Provincial governments are unnecessary middlemen, too big to handle the little things, generally speaking, and too small to cope with the big things. The provincial power base must be pulled apart from both ends, with certain responsibilities assumed by the federal government and the remainder — the majority — devolved to the new localities. As a result, a level of costly and clumsy bureaucracy will be eliminated, and greater control over their own destiny will be given to Canadians. Calls for aboriginal self-government could be substantially met through such measures, the continued search for a unified though multicultural mosaic furthered, and the threat of separation and collapse forever removed. Edmonton, Whitby, or Cape Breton would not have the desire or the means to form independent governments, whereas Quebec, Alberta, or British Columbia most certainly would.

Though such reform may seem radical at first glance, it is painfully evident that such measures are needed. Our institutions have fallen behind our ideals, and rather than helping us reach our goals, such outmoded machinery is only serving to hinder. Lines in the sand must not be permitted to rip this nation apart.

Related to this approach of localism is the need to renew a sense of *equality* among all Canadians. Though the nine players on a baseball team occupy significantly different positions, all are part of a unified whole. A winning team relies on the combined sum of its individual components, each recognizing the fact that they all play on the same field. Similarly, on our national playing field, every individual needs a sense of shared responsibility, and in turn must be rewarded for his or her contribution to the team effort. To paraphrase George Orwell, a hierarchical society is only possible on a foundation of poverty and ignorance. In Canada, such a society has been fostered by an extremely hierarchical political system.

Even the most conservative of analysts must acknowledge that a nation in which resides a permanent class of "have-nots" cannot reach its full potential. With the localist approach adopted, the lack of enterprise and education that has led to the formation of this underclass could be mitigated and given much more constructive and creative attention. Through the nurturing of a grassroots democratic process, via referendums and other means of popular governance, political efficacy will be encouraged and the black cloud of ignorance lifted. With the sense that they are contributing members of the whole, those who find themselves members of this underclass today will evolve into productive members of society tomorrow. At the very least, an equality of opportunity should be guaranteed.

Of course, active participation in government will not yield overnight or complete results. Explicit efforts must be made to lift this segment of the population into the mainstream, through education, retraining, and similar social programs. In this age of intense scrutiny on spending, not a single dollar can be wasted — social levelling must be achieved not by bringing the top down but by bringing the bottom up. And so, it is clearly more prudent to invest a little more now in each individual, in the hopes of minimizing expense in the future. Through this combination of localism and enlightened social intervention, and upon seeing the worth of themselves, individuals can become productive citizens of Canada.

A critical component of this entire equalization process, and one in which government must play a key role, is job creation. There is little point in providing manufacturing training to the fishermen of Newfoundland unless Magna International, for example, is willing to set up shop in St. John's. Incentives to do so must be offered, and in this age of globalization, a balance must be sought and a game of brinkmanship played, ensuring industrial commitment and contribution to Canada while not stifling growth.

The current and divisive practice of one province plundering the jobs of another is counter-productive, yielding no net national gain. Simply moving employment is not creating employment. Thus, it is the *federal* government that must foster both the attraction of multinational corporations and the establishment of small business (supported by local initiatives), the two most vital components of any job creation strategy. One or two jobs here and there, combined with a periodic shot in the arm from a major development, should provide a balanced and fruitful approach to job creation.

Finally, hand in hand with this new productivity, a sincere appreciation of the *environment* must be maintained. When discussing the standard of living, it is important to remember that there is more to it than dollars and cents. To be certain, economic well-being and prosperity are intrinsic parts of the equation; however, such goals must be kept in balance with environmental realities if an optimum quality of life is to be obtained.

Unfortunately, the term "environment" has taken on a far narrower meaning of late than it should. Certainly critical to Canadians, and indeed all the people of the planet, is the natural environment. Equally important, however, are the distinctly human creations within which we work, grow, and play ball. While natural grass and blue skies add immensely to the vista offered from the left-field bleachers, the ballpark itself can be improved and perfected, and must not be forgotten. The same follows for the cities we live in and the roofs over our heads.

Thus, it is imperative that the federal government, in conjunction with the new localities, take a complete approach to the environment in order to improve not only the standard of living for all Canadians but their place of living as well. Few things impact more greatly upon a society than its surroundings, with everything from crime rates to health levels being influenced by our total "environment." And so, attention must be given to greening our cities, reinvigorating our downtowns, and revitalizing our communities, aided by the aforementioned localist and equality pillars of reform.

Only when all Canadians can call a particular space "home" with pride will this nation reach its full potential. Having something to work for will further the equalization process; having something to protect will advance the spirit of community. Here government, particularly municipal government, can have a most beneficial influence.

Therefore, it is apparent that the three tenets most clearly espoused through this discussion — localism, equality, and environment — are strongly interrelated, each one necessary if the other two are to be realized. Through an integrated approach, it is possible for government to further all three, and in turn improve the situation of each individual Canadian and of the nation as a whole. Despite the current reputation of government, whether deserved or not, there must be a recognition that there is still the opportunity to reform, to improve, and to perfect.

Of course, these three canons alone will not produce such a society, and there are innumerable other measures that could, and should, be pursued to ensure its realization.

Laws must embody the social values of Canada, and through such an embodiment inspire adherence to them. Catering only to a particular segment of society is not advantageous. Instead, at the federal level, laws must approach as nearly as possible a level of universality, and those laws of a more divisive nature should be left for localities to decide for themselves. The needs of a Toronto stockbroker and of a Prairie farmer are entirely different, and likewise their social values. The lawmakers of Canada must acknowledge this fact and attempt to minimize such differences rather than aggravate them.

Culture is as much a part of a nation, and of nation-building, as constitutions and civil codes. Furthering the creative inspirations of Canadians is a necessary role of government in order to foster both continued individual and national growth. Art, music, literature, and sport should all be encouraged, increasing prosperity in its broadest sense and consequently generating a feeling of unity.

And in line with the previous call for an increasingly responsive government, the installation of an electoral system based on proportional representation should be considered. As can be witnessed in the current House of Commons, the allocation of seats does not coincide with the beliefs of Canadians, who may see little value in a political system where separatists can become the Official Opposition, only because something is lost in the transition from ballot box to political reality. The Senate, too, should be made more representative, particularly of the distinct regions of Canada.

Some might discount such proposals as wishful thinking, an

espousal of a social utopia in an age of rightist thought and division. But with care and effort we can achieve such goals, together.

For too long have we tinkered, satisfied with a "muddling through" approach to politics. We have not taken true advantage of what we are fully able to achieve. Dramatic reform has been stifled as too risky, while virtually all facets of society have become tarnished under the tenure of the status quo. Clearly, the status quo is no longer good enough.

Ordinary Canadians, often left out of the political process, have much to contribute. Instead of spending the entire game on the bench, every citizen of Canada should be given a chance to go to bat. The current system rests on the principle of waste, not only of resources and opportunities, but of talent simply waiting to be tapped. Our problems are solvable, difficult as they may be. We simply have to be willing to listen to some innovative solutions.

For those who still do not recognize the potential value of the particular solutions offered herein, Switzerland could easily be upheld as a model of what Canada could be. Through local and popular control, a diverse country with four official languages has managed to pass through centuries intact. As we look forward to a new century, we must pursue the goal of a united and prosperous future, a dream entirely within the realm of possibility, if only we are willing to take the chance and achieve our full potential as a nation.

With one mighty swing of the bat, we may all find ourselves, once again, safe at home.

SIX

Canadian "Victim Syndrome": A Chronic Case of False Modesty

• • • • • • • • • • •
AUDREY SATTELBERGER-LAPORTE

A udrey is entering her first year of a Ph.D. program in the Department of Economics at the University of Guelph in Ontario. As a master's student at the University of Guelph, she co-wrote an academic paper with the chair of the Department of Economics. Audrey is a former member of the Executive Council of the North American Model United Nations centred at the University of Toronto, where she was also involved in the Hart House Debating Society. Audrey worked for five years as a ward clerk in the emergency department of Etobicoke General Hospital in Toronto to help finance her education.

WHEN SIR WILFRID LAURIER PROCLAIMED THAT "THE twentieth century belongs to Canada," he recognized the tremendous potential of his country. Indeed, Canada's small population, equipped with a vast storehouse of natural resources and straddling the most vigorous economy in the world, seemed destined to live in unprecedented prosperity. Although Canadians are wealthy by world standards, there is ample evidence to indicate that we as a nation have fallen short of this early expectation.

Family incomes are at 1985 levels, having fallen by 6 percent over the last six years. Our governments, unable to balance the budget over a long period of time, have allowed the debt to reach astronomical proportions. The Canadian dollar, relative to the currencies of some first-rate economies, has fallen by 70 percent over two decades. Today, 2.5 million of our citizens are on social assistance while 1.4 million are unemployed. We also face the possible secession of Quebec from the

Canadian federation, increasing further the uncertainty about our economic and political prospects.

To make matters worse, there is a widespread condition in the country, fostered by politicians and the media, that can be described as "victim syndrome." From this viewpoint, all of our problems can be traced to outside forces: financial markets are responsible for the high level of interest rates; unemployment is the result of too many immigrants; the dollar is losing its value because of unscrupulous money traders; and recessions are the result of a weak American economy. With this type of mentality we have allowed ourselves to become uncompetitive and unimaginative, preferring to be *reactive* rather than *pro-active*. There is no clear vision or strategy on the part of decision-makers to harness the inherent strengths of this country. As prime minister, I would bring an end to this malaise by tapping into the ingenuity of the population and seeking innovative and viable solutions where they are most likely to be found — at home.

The policies outlined hereafter assume that national unity questions are inseparable from economic considerations. For, in the end, the longevity and prosperity of our federation rest on its capacity to deliver a high living standard while respecting the cultural and regional diversity of its people.

Laying the Foundations...

The dynamics of the modern marketplace have shifted from boom-and-bust natural resource industries to knowledge-based, software-driven companies. This new environment calls for a partnership between government, industry, labour, the investment community, and the educational establishment. To achieve long-term success, *governmental economic policy must support institutions and entrepreneurs that generate wealth through technological progress*.

Many companies have for decades obscured inefficiencies in their operations. Capital assets, for example, are written off at historical rather than replacement cost, allowing business to report inflated profits. Furthermore, since Canada produces few of these capital goods, they are imported for the most part from countries with relatively strong currencies. As a result, many companies cannot afford to upgrade equipment to stay competitive and turn instead to cheap labour as the equalizer. The social costs and revenue impact of this low-wage job policy are just now being acknowledged. Returns on investment in the non-financial sector have been inadequate for two decades, while job turnovers are running at ten times the level of Japan and Europe, reflecting low productivity and falling investment. Considering that of twenty-three newly registered companies on the TSE 300 in January only two can be classified as "high-tech," it appears that the transition to the "new economy" is far from complete in Canada.[1] We are losing the competitive edge we need to be a first-rung industrial power.

This need not be the case. Canadian entrepreneurs cannot hope to compete if they are deprived of the three fundamental inputs of modern business: capital, skilled labour, and advanced technology. Unfortunately, interest rate adjustment is the government's favoured tool to control inflation and attract foreign investment. This short-term approach favours holders of financial assets but inhibits innovation in existing domestic industries and stifles the creation of small and medium-sized corporations. *The government must promote increases in productivity (the true hedge against inflation) by giving companies access to the three inputs they require.*

1. Access to capital

We rely excessively on foreign capital to develop our economy. Fully one-third of it is foreign-controlled, reducing the government's ability to forge a common industrial policy that benefits all Canadians. We can take the initiative in the diversification of the economy by cultivating an environment that fosters the creation and growth of home-grown transnational corporations. Of the one hundred largest transnationals, ranked by revenue, Canada boasts only three, whereas Sweden and Switzerland, with a fraction of our population, have five and six, respectively. Transnationals can be an important vehicle for diversifying our industrial base because they use hundreds, if not thousands, of independent niche suppliers for products and services. These large corporations can contribute to the establishment of a stable workforce and may even help some of their suppliers to grow into transnationals themselves.

The government can encourage this process by spearheading the drive to broaden the lending base for new ventures in small to medium-sized companies in high-tech sectors such as biotechnology, micro-electronics, mechanical engineering, and robotics. This can be done in concert with the Canada Development Corporation and the Federal Business Development Bank (FBDB). For the FBDB to be effective, however, it must be a provider of start-up financing for companies in these designated areas rather than a lender of last resort for all types of businesses. In addition, other non-deposit-taking financial institutions specializing in knowledge-based lending should be made part of the Small Business Loans Insurance Act without having to be members of the Canadian Payments Association. This will give entrepreneurs an alternative to the conservative, formula-based lending policies of our banks.

More effective use can be made of the government's $6 billion in "science and technology" funds, of which $3.6 billion goes to the Canada Research Council (CRC), leaving $2.4 billion going directly to the private sector before it is administered by sixty different government departments. These funds can be integrated to a larger extent with universities, having the CRC set strategic goals while the funds are administered by a private sector advisory board composed of academics and representatives from the business community.

2. Access to skilled labour

To develop a successful strategy of diversification, we must recognize that investment in our human resources is vital. Although at first glance Canada's job creation record appears satisfactory, a closer look reveals that most job creation is in low-wage sectors. From 1981 to 1990 the sub-$8/hour wage category accounted for 78 percent of Canada's job growth, while all other categories declined.[2] In fact, the percentage of the labour force earning less than $20,000 annually rose from 46.8 percent in 1981 to 51 percent in 1990. Moreover, these low-wage workers are more than three times as likely than high-wage workers to draw unemployment insurance, and they remain out of work longer.[3] If this trend persists, tax revenues will continue to be outstripped by an ever-increasing need for support payments, making it virtually impossible to balance the budget.

It is therefore puzzling that most reform-minded officials limit their ideas to cutting social programs, considering that in fiscal year 1996–97 social spending will be at 10.4 percent of GDP, the same level seen in 1949–50, when there was no medicare or unemployment insurance.

The truth is that we will be deficit-plagued so long as a low-skill, low-wage job creation policy is pursued — unless, of course, we are willing to sacrifice our social net. I believe that Canadians need not accept such an outcome.

With high secondary school drop-out rates, and 60 percent of students who do enter university not finishing with a degree, it is clear that our education system, at least at the pre-university level, does not produce enough of the skilled labour Canada requires. As prime minister, I would see as a *top* priority the freeing of revenues within the education bureaucracy that contribute nothing to the quality of our workforce. At present, 54 percent of education funds at the pre-university level are spent on bureaucracy, leaving only 46 percent for classroom spending. That ratio should be changed to 25 percent for administration and 75 percent for the classroom.

Although education falls under provincial jurisdiction, skill levels can be improved by adopting strict federal standards with regard to math, science, and language curricula. In addition, we need re-certification requirements for teachers and end-of-year standardized exams for students, such as those proposed by the recent Royal Commission on Education in Ontario. Adopting strict national standards, reflecting the needs of the marketplace and of our leading universities, would make most school boards redundant, thereby achieving significant savings in education costs.

3. Access to technology
The partnership between industry and the education establishment is key to providing the private sector with the skilled labour and technology necessary to insure its competitiveness. One possibility is the expansion of co-operative programs, which expose students to the practical know-how of corporations. Universities and our industrial sector need to be integrated more fully by sharing their collective intellectual and scientific capacities through licensing agreements for processes or patent transfers. Canadian universities combined derive only $8 million annually from such sources, less than one prominent American institution by itself. Instead of publishing floods of theoretical papers that gather dust, this valuable knowledge could earn income for teaching institutions and be of great benefit to the private sector.

For a More Equitable and Dynamic Canada

It should by now be apparent that there are profound imbalances affecting our economic performance. In 1985 the Macdonald Royal Commission found that certain sectors in our economy derive more from it than they contribute. Since then, successive studies have shown that public sector wages, for example, are at least 20 percent higher than for comparable work in the private sector. This kind of institutionalized privilege can only be maintained through the excessive taxation of productive sectors.

Not only do private sector workers earn significantly less on average than their counterparts in the civil service, they must also contend with greater economic insecurity. While a recession has meant that many civil servants accept early retirement or a few days off a year without pay, for a great number of Canadian workers it has meant job loss and the dreadful possibility of losing their homes. When one considers that one in five Canadians is employed by public agencies, the magnitude of this kind of wealth transfer becomes clear. My government would ensure that public and private sector wages eventually converge.

Another way to streamline the operations of our civil service is to *implement a simplified tax-collection regime.* This structural reform is four-pronged. First, our tax base can be broadened while tax rates are slightly reduced. Second, Revenue Canada can collect all corporate taxes for the provinces, while provincial revenue ministries collect all personal income tax and levies. The total amount of funds collected and distributed would remain unchanged. Each province may list its own exceptions. Provincial and federal taxation jurisdictions will be preserved, while collection administration costs will be reduced. Third, a uniform national sales tax, replacing our dual system, can be introduced and collected by Ottawa.[4] Finally, the non-income-based capital tax can increase from its current 0.2 percent to 0.3 percent for corporations with taxable capital in excess of $1 billion, as income-based taxes are reduced by 25 percent for all corporations.

There are many other initiatives that can rationalize administration costs and reduce the burden on taxpayers and consumers. Since Canadian businesses are still burdened with $50 billion in regulatory and compliance costs, a blue-ribbon task force, with a mandate to find a framework to reduce these costs by an initial 20 percent, should be established forthwith, and its findings implemented. The recent initiatives by the federal government to divest itself of Canadian National and Petro-Canada are welcome but could also include an amalgamation of the ministries of Natural Resources, the Environment, and Fisheries. Furthermore, our country finds itself part of a North American free trade zone, yet interprovincial barriers, costing consumers billions of dollars, are still to a large extent in place. The federal authorities must speed up the multilateral negotiations that will eliminate these barriers.

With this streamlining under way, my cabinet will deal with an issue that ties national unity questions to economic problems: the nature of equalization payments between Ottawa and the provinces. Although at the time of inception the policy of equalization payments was perceived as essential for national development, it has had very limited success. Many of the net-recipient provinces still depend on these funds after twenty-five years. The lack of co-ordination between partners and the absence of a coherent industrial policy have imposed heavy costs on our country, straining relations between its various parts. The difficulties experienced in our fisheries have highlighted the effects of such governmental mismanagement. It now costs $3 billion a year for the buying out of commercial licences to fund retraining and compensation for job losses. Canada declared in 1977 a two-hundred-mile economic development zone around its coastlines; if, at the time, a small landing fee for each ton of fish caught had been imposed and applied towards the establishment of a fish-farming industry, resources would have been spared and employment maintained. Norway has done just that, selling $2 billion worth of farm-raised fish on the export market in 1994, creating 14,000 jobs in the process. Had such a collaborative strategy been pursued in Canada, not only would we have experienced positive economic effects (i.e., maintaining jobs and reducing the dependency on federal transfer payments), we would have been able to preserve the regional and cultural integrity of life on the East Coast.

A collaborative approach can be applied to reduce our $4.5-billion travel deficit with the rest of the world. Many of our citizens travel regularly to the United States but have never visited another province. As a result, alienation between regions continues to weaken national bonds. To break the cycle of mistrust, I would build upon the excellent infrastructure already in place by encouraging co-operation between Parks

Canada, the ministries of Tourism, and transportation companies, thereby promoting travel by Canadians in Canada.

It is a crisis of leadership that in large measure explains the widespread discontent felt in Quebec, and in other parts of the country. We must break free of reactive and short-sighted policies that erode the legacy of our forefathers. We find ourselves at a crucial crossroads. Yet, it is not too late for us to prepare for the challenges that lie ahead. It is not too late to guarantee that the twenty-first century belongs to Canada.

Notes

1. The majority of the other corporations were traditional oil and gas producers and companies servicing the resource sector. Statistic quoted in "The Bottom Line" series by Deirdre McMurdy.

2. Except for the $16/hour to $23/hour category, which increased a mere 0.4 percent.

3. These statistics are quoted from J. Meyer's *Globe and Mail* article: "Focus on quality of jobs not just on the quantity," April 1995.

4. It would be integrated into the price of the products sold.

SEVEN

A NEW MAGNA CARTA: A NEW APPROACH FOR A NEW CANADA

• • • • • • • • • •
E. STEPHEN JOHNSON

orn in Toronto, Stephen is currently completing his doctorate on the Comparative Politics of Industrialized Nations. He currently works as a teaching assistant in the Department of Economics at the University of Toronto, where he is president of the Graduate Students' Union. He is also a past chair of the National Graduate Council, Canadian Federation of Students, and past president of the Canadian University Society for intercollegiate debate. He is the winner of more than seventy national and international awards for debating and public speaking.

AS PRIME MINISTER I WOULD HAVE FORMIDABLE RESOURCES to use to unify Canada and improve the living standards of its people. When backed by a majority in the House of Commons, convention gives the prime minister the power to direct the executive and legislative power of the entire national government.

The prime minister's political power lies in his or her leadership of a political party, whose members of Parliament have often been elected "on the coat-tails" of a popular leader who is also the focus of public and media attention. This focus is a source of strength as it allows the prime minister a means of communicating directly with the people. I would use this platform to remind Canadians of our past and focus their thinking about our future. Once a month I would host an open-line radio or TV "town hall" to give the people the chance to address senior ministers directly. In addition, I would write a weekly newspaper column that the press could publish. This use of the media would demystify the office and help me explain the goals sought by my government.

National unity is a fundamental challenge confronting every prime minister. In the nineteenth century Sir Georges Étienne Cartier noted that Canadians needed to create a political nationality. The temple for this new nation would be supported by the twin pillars of parliamentary constitutionalism and federalism. In practice, these pillars have been perceived as walls that separate us rather than the foundations of the home we all share. To understand how this has happened we must recognize the fundamental tension between constitutional and communal views of society and nation-building.

Constitutionalist views hope that the unity of the nation will be secured by the procedures and rights defined in the constitution, which are meant to create unity out of conflicting interests, identities, and opinions. Communalist views hold the belief that procedural fairness alone cannot replace societal consensus and participation as the bases of a unified nation. Each of our pillars supports procedures as the basis for unity, but, in practice, these procedures reinforce pre-existing disunity.

For example, the "winner-takes-all" electoral system creates parliamentary governments without majority popular support. It has not been uncommon for the voters of entire provinces to be unrepresented by the governing party. Years of exclusion from the governments of the 1970s bred resentment in the West, and the prominence of Quebec's representatives in every government since 1945 (except 1957–58) has led many Canadians to believe that Quebec gets preferential treatment. Our electoral system also distorts the Canadian reality by under-representing women, visible minorities, aboriginal peoples, and the physically challenged. I would adopt the German electoral model, by which half of an expanded three-hundred-member House of Commons would be elected as they are now and the other half elected on the basis of proportional representation. This second half would be selected according to the results of an additional ballot that Canadians would cast at election time, allowing them to choose their preferred party. If a party won over 5 percent of the national vote it would be entitled to representation. If my party won 40 percent on this second ballot, my party would name sixty members of Parliament. Of these I would ensure that at least thirty were women, and I would guarantee that every province and territory was represented in my government. Constituencies would be larger and every Canadian would still have "their" member of Parliament. This would ensure that no future government would lack representation from a province, and it would transform parliamentary debate into a chorus of Canada's many voices.

The parliamentary system also breeds public resentment when people see their representatives silenced by the demands of party. I would declare all budgetary and financial issues to be party votes and all other issues to be free votes. And I would surrender the prime minister's power over the timing of elections by committing my government to go to the polls fifty-four months after the election.

Finally, I would improve Parliament's other voice by modifying the Senate. I would amend section 29 of the constitution to end the practice of having senators sit until age seventy-five and replace it with a term of office equal to the life of two Parliaments. When appointing senators I would honour the results of the previous election and ensure that my appointments consisted of members of all political parties. Finally, I would delay appointments until most provinces had only six senators. Ontario's and Quebec's representation would be allowed to fall to twelve and I would ensure that six were from each of Toronto and Montreal. This design would make the Senate into a potentially effective counter to the central Canadian majority in the House. If re-elected, I would propose a constitutional amendment and invite the provinces to ratify this new Senate.

Canadians often equate the term "federal" with "national," so that a "federalist" is one who supports the national government. Debates about federalism often revolve around the implicit demand that citizens choose Canada as their primary loyalty. This is precisely what federalism is designed to counter! Federalism is meant to protect and develop provincial and national identities. In the same way that I should not ask my wife to choose my family over hers, I would encourage Canadians to recognize that they can love their national family without betraying their provincial home.

I would take steps to recognize the aboriginal and francophone communities in Canada. I would endorse aboriginal self-government and eliminate the Department of Indian Affairs. The native budget and the former department's powers would be handed over to band governments, as was done in Manitoba in 1994. Turning to Quebec, I would recognize the province's fear that its unique cultural identity will be lost as its share of the population declines. I would give Quebec full control over its immigration and ask Parliament to formally recognize Quebec's unique interest in language policy within its borders.

Reforms to Parliament and alterations to the practice of federalism can only affect the way in which Canadians speak with a common vote. How they build a better standard of living involves policy, and it is in this area that my government would be the most active. Its initiatives would address: the physical environment we share; the safety we deserve in our communities; the social welfare of our least advantaged people; the families we build; the economy we want to build; and the debts that threaten our children's future.

I would initiate legislation to reward manufacturers who use recycled material by giving them a higher GST credit. If their products used 51 to 74 percent recycled material, my government would add 10 percent to their rebate. The use of 75 to 99 percent and 100 percent recycled material would, respectively, earn the producer an extra 20 percent and 30 percent. Conversely, those using 0 to 10 percent, 11 to 20 percent, 21 to 30 percent, 31 to 40 percent, and 41 to 50 percent would receive rebates 40 percent, 30 percent, 20 percent, and 10 percent lower than their entitlement. Using the same GST rebate formula, my government would join with industry to set packaging standards and reward or punish companies according to their compliance with these standards, starting one year after their introduction.

I would join with industry to set emission standards for each industrial sector, and then create a market for the environment by giving annual credits to companies that met these standards. A company that met this standard would receive 150 credits whereas one that did not would receive none. Companies with 100 credits would be taxed at the regular corporate tax rate while those without enough credits would be taxed along the following scale: 0 credits equals 200 percent; 99 credits equals 101 percent. Money raised by the extra tax would be dedicated to a National Clean-Up and Mass Transit Fund, and as the sectors improved the standards would be revised until all companies met them.

Protection of the environment also includes the protection of the man-made environment, and this inevitably leads to the Criminal Code. On legal issues, my government would focus on the *perception* of justice. This involves the fact that sentencing is not uniform across the country. My government would bring uniformity with common sentences, so that the same crime warrants the same punishment. I would also propose that the possession of a firearm in the commission of a crime involve a mandatory twenty-five-year sentence. Violent or repeat sexual offenders would receive mandatory life sentences without the possibility of parole. Finally, the Young Offenders Act would be reformed so that it applied only upon the recommendation of a judge or upon the agreement of the crown and the defence. In this way, the act would facilitate the rehabilitation of misguided youth without giving some a licence to commit crime.

The natural and built environments constitute the realm in which people's personal lives are conducted and enriched. Essential to this enrichment is time for family. I would follow the French example and legislate that all people be entitled to four weeks paid vacation, and, following European models, my government would provide two years of paid parental and adoption leave. Recognizing the reality of working-parent families, these initiatives would represent state recognition of the primacy of family and facilitate this with a four-year program to build $8 billion worth of public day-care.

This leads to the question of social welfare and public pensions. Our pension system is a patchwork of programs that account for billions in public expenditure without meeting the solid policy objective of providing for the disadvantaged. A "pay as you go" system, the Canada Pension Plan (CPP) is not a pension that today's retirees have "earned" through contributions. Rather, it is an actuarially unsound intergenerational tax that cannot be sustained when the "baby-boom" generation reaches retirement age. Moreover, with the exception of the Guaranteed Income Supplement, present pension programs are not social welfare programs designed to save the elderly from the indignity of poverty, as demonstrated by the fact that almost 30 percent of today's recipients have incomes above the national average. In addition to taxing the young, the current pension scheme uses registered retirement savings plans (RRSPs) to encourage today's "boomers" to accumulate capital for their retirement.

I would fundamentally alter social programs by rolling unemployment insurance (UI) and CPP premiums into a single fund and eliminating both of these programs. The CPP Investment Fund would be liquidated and used to endow 14,000 Canadian chairs in universities. Each chair would be endowed with $3 million to be invested in the Canadian economy. Assuming an annual return of 5 percent, this $42 billion would generate $2.1 billion for Canadian universities and replace the $2.1 billion in federal post-secondary education support. Tax revenue used for Old Age Security, spousal allowances, and the post-secondary education and Canada Assistance Plan transfers to the provinces would also be added to this single fund, thus redirecting $55.7 billion into a new Guaranteed Annual Income Program (GAI). A further $1.25 billion would be added to personal income tax by eliminating the existing pension and age credits, with at least a further $1.75 billion being added by converting RRSP contributions into non-refundable tax credits. All told, this new fund would total $58.7 billion ($55.7 billion in redirected programming and $3 billion in new tax revenue) and would be modelled on the Australian pension scheme.

Every Canadian citizen above the age of eighteen would annually receive $10,000 in monthly cheques. Fifty cents would be deducted and repaid through the tax system for every dollar in additional income that the recipient made. Thus, someone earning $20,000 would receive no GAI. The 1992 taxation statistics show that 2.95 million taxpayers earned between $10,000 and $15,000. If we apply this to 1995–96 and assume that all of these people made only $10,000, then each would be entitled to a GAI of ($10,000 − ($10,000 × 50 percent)), or $5,000, which amounts to nearly $580 million. The GAI would amount to $64.6 billion if we applied this assumption to the 10,243,964 Canadians who reported income up to $20,000 in 1992. If one uses the middle income from each range and, for example, assumes that the 2.95 million reporting $10–15,000 earn $12,500, then the total cost of the GAI is reduced to $59.5 billion. Taking the average of these two figures, my government would budget $62 billion for this program in addition to the $4.4-billion cost of retaining the Old Age Income Supplement. The GAI would provide citizens with money to assist their education, their retirement, their child-care expenses, or it could act as a simple supplement to their low-wage jobs. The GAI would replace all federal-provincial shared-cost programs, except health care, which would be partially funded by $2 billion generated by a 5 percent surtax on those with income in excess of $40,000.

No government subsidy can replace productive work in the private sector. To encourage job growth I would eliminate the $11.5 billion in UI premiums and approximately $4.9 billion in CPP premiums paid by employers and the $8.2 billion in UI and $4.9 billion in CPP premiums deducted from employees' paycheques. To replace all of the $9.76 billion in foregone CPP revenue, all of the UI revenue from employees, and 80 percent of the UI revenue from employers (total $27.13 billion), I would place a 43 percent surtax on personal income tax. This approach would also be a form of progressive taxation as the upper 20 percent of all income-earners would come to pay close to 70 percent of the total raised to replace CPP and UI premiums. Similarly, to replace the remaining 20 percent of the UI revenue from employers (total $2.3 billion), a 15 percent surtax on corporate income tax would be levied. The net result would be a saving to employers of approximately $14.1 billion, which, after the elimination of $2.5 billion in business subsidies, would leave the private sector with $11.1 billion to reinvest in the economy.

Despite my budget's $20.2 billion operating surplus,[1] the anticipated $49.5-billion cost to service the national debt of $546 billion would result in a deficit of $29.3 billion. The challenge of the debt leads many to advocate the reduction of services and the passing on of greater costs to future generations. I would oppose this thinking and stipulate that those responsible for the debt should be the ones to pay for it. The current national debt has its roots in the mid-1970s, and very little of it was accumulated to build the country. Years of interest on government bonds has caused the debt to grow, especially as interest rates have been allowed to rise, both to attract foreign capital and to protect the value of the Canadian dollar. The people who have benefited the most from the debt are those who had their peak earning years over the past twenty-five years and now buy government bonds as part of their retirement investments. In addition, these "baby-boomers" had the benefit of government pensions for their parents, which freed them from the traditional obligation of financing or at least supplementing their parents' retirement.

In addition to federal debt, each province has an accumulated debt, and together the provinces owe close to $300 billion. Canada is the only major federation that allows unlimited provincial borrowing. In the

United States, forty-nine states have some kind of balanced-budget law; Australian state borrowing is centrally co-ordinated; and German *Lander* cannot even raise their own taxes. As prime minister, I would offer to assume provincial debts in return for a common national sales tax to be set at 14 percent, which would generate $17.5 billion for the federal government.

The assumption of provincial debt would lead to a deficit of $38.9 billion, assuming an annual debt servicing cost equal to 9.1 percent of the combined debt of $846 billion. I would address this by altering the rules governing private pension funds and by introducing a mandatory retirement savings program modelled on the current RRSP program. These reforms would free capital for domestic investment by restricting tax-credit-eligible pension funds to domestic investment. Furthermore, recognizing that these pension funds are the debt-creating generation's retirement investment fund, sheltered by tax credits and accumulated during the past twenty-five years of debt accumulation, I would require some of this accumulated capital to be used to reduce the existing burden of financing the accumulated debt. This would be accomplished by introducing legislation comparable to that used during World War I and World War II, which would require private funds to invest 5 percent of their holdings in special Canada Savings Bonds with an interest rate tied to inflation.

The second means of financing and repaying the debt would be through a new mandatory RRSP program, which would require all taxpayers above the age of forty-five to purchase $2,500 in government "retirement bonds" until the age of seventy. Like the special Canada Savings Bonds to be purchased by private pension funds, these bonds would have an interest rate tied to inflation.

The government would then be faced with three options. The mandatory RRSP program could offer bonds tied to inflation (assuming a rate of 3 percent per year) and run surpluses until the debt is paid in the year 2017. The second option could see the program run until 2006, after which time market rates of up to 9.1 percent per year could be paid and sustained, as enough of the debt would have been retired to allow the budget to carry this cost. The final option, and the one that I would endorse, would provide a retirement program that would both break the cycle of debt and provide Canadians with a superior return.

If every Canadian taxpayer invested $2,500 at 9.1 percent for the next twenty-five years, the accumulated interest would amount to $172,000. The program I would present would involve a twenty-five-year government retirement RRSP that would pay 3 percent for the first twelve years, 6 percent for years thirteen and fourteen, 12 percent for years fifteen through seventeen, and 15 percent for the final eight years, generating $183,720 in interest after twenty-five years, which would be tax-free upon maturity.

Regardless of the chosen model, the new approach to tax-favoured retirement savings plans would generate annual budget surpluses of at least $12.3 billion per year. Assuming annual inflation of 3 percent and a similar rate of growth in revenue and expenditure I, as prime minister, would have created a budgetary regime capable of eliminating the national and provincial debts by the year 2017, or at least capable of reversing the cycle of debt accumulation by the year 2006. An equitable and compassionate model, this approach to the nation's finances and future would promote rather than sacrifice the nation's unity, environment, and social welfare for our future generations.

TABLE 1:

Budget Model Compared to 1995-96 Federal Budget

	Federal Budget	Proposal
Personal Income Tax	$60,339,600,000	$60,339,600,000
UI Employee	$8,214,000,000	$0
*CPP Employee	$4,860,000,000	$0
GAI Personal Surtax	$0	$27,133,680,000
Corporate Income Tax	$15,451,200,000	$15,451,200,000
UI Employer	$11,499,600,000	$0
CPP Employer	$4,860,000,000	$0
GAI Corporate Surtax	$0	$2,299,920,000
GST	$17,449,200,000	$17,449,200,000
Provincial Sales Tax	$0	$17,449,200,000
Sales/Excise	$12,520,800,000	$12,520,800,000
Other	$7,725,600,000	$7,725,600,000
End Pension Credit	$0	$1,000,000,000

	Federal Budget	Proposal
End Age Credit	$0	$250,000,000
RRSP as Credit	$0	$1,750,000,000
Health Surtax	$0	$1,900,000,000
SUB-TOTAL	**$142,920,000,000**	**$165,269,200,000**
Non-Budget Transactions	$7,800,000,000	$7,800,000,000
TOTAL REVENUE	**$150,720,000,000**	**$173,069,200,000**
Guaranteed Annual Income	$0	$62,000,000,000
UI	$14,300,000,000	$0
OAS	$16,400,000,000	$0
GIS	$4,400,000,000	$4,400,000,000
OAS-SA	$400,000,000	$0
Veterans	$1,800,000,000	$1,800,000,000
CPP	$14,940,000,000	$0
SUB-TOTAL	**$52,240,000,000**	**$68,200,000,000**
Health	$6,700,000,000	$6,700,000,000
PSE	$2,100,000,000	$0
CAP	$7,400,000,000	$0
Equalization	$8,900,000,000	$8,900,000,000
Territories	$1,000,000,000	$1,000,000,000
SUB-TOTAL	**$26,100,000,000**	**$16,600,000,000**
Business Subsidies	$2,500,000,000	$0
Natives	$4,000,000,000	$4,000,000,000
International Aid	$2,200,000,000	$2,200,000,000
Science & Technology	$900,000,000	$900,000,000
Infrastructure	$800,000,000	$0
Day-care Program	$0	$2,000,000,000
Other	$5,000,000,000	$5,000,000,000
SUB-TOTAL	**$15,400,000,000**	**$14,100,000,000**
Defence	$10,300,000,000	$10,300,000,000
Crown Corporations	$4,500,000,000	$4,500,000,000
Government Operations	$19,200,000,000	$19,200,000,000
SUB-TOTAL	**$34,000,000,000**	**$34,000,000,000**
Reserve	$2,500,000,000	$2,500,000,000
TOTAL PROGRAMS	**$130,240,000,000**	**$135,400,000,000**

	Federal Budget	Proposal
OPERATING SURPLUS	$20,480,000,000	$37,669,200,000
Federal Debt @ 9.1%	$49,500,000,000	$0
Federal Debt @ 3%	$0	$16,380,000,000
Provincial Debt @ 3%	$0	$9,000,000,000
TOTAL EXPENSES	$179,740,000,000	$160,780,000,000
Deficit/Surplus	−$29,020,000,000	$12,289,200,000
1996 Federal Debt	$575,020,000,000	$538,012,020,000
1996 Provincial Debt	$300,000,000,000	$295,698,780,000

*The CPP contributions shown here are not items contained in the federal budget but have been included for purposes of comparison.

Options:

1. Run surpluses until debt paid in 2017.
2. Run surpluses until 2006 and resume market rates, having broken the back of the debt, and allow it to be carried at market rates up to 9.1 percent.
3. Offer a special series of twenty-five-year "retirement programs" with 3 percent for the first twelve years (1995–2006); 6 percent for the next two years (2007–08); 12 percent for the next three years (2009–12); and 15 percent for the final eight years. This system would require annual contributions of $2,500 and, after twenty-five years, generate a total of $183,720 in interest. In contrast, investing $2,500 each year at 9.1 percent generates $172,000.

Impact of Fiscal Changes and Guaranteed Annual Income (not including provincial taxes)

Single Pensioners

CURRENT: receive OAS and GIS receives $9,951. KEEP: $9,951
CURRENT: receive 1/2 CPP, OAS, GIS = $11,953. KEEP: $11,600
CURRENT: receive full CPP, OAS, GIS = $13,956. KEEP: $13,253
PROPOSAL: receive $10,000 GAI and $5,404 GIS. KEEP: $11,528

Pensioner Couple

CURRENT: receive OAS and GIS receives $16,137. KEEP: $16,087
CURRENT: receive 1/2 CPP, OAS, GIS = $18,139. KEEP: $17,739

CURRENT: receive full CPP, OAS, GIS = $20,141. KEEP: $19,391
PROPOSAL: receive $20,000 GAI and $7,043 GIS. KEEP: $21,728

Working Poor

$13,000 (minimum wage: $6.25/hr) with $2,340 RRSP contribution
CURRENT: Federal tax and CPP/UI premiums: $1,274. KEEP: $11,726
PROPOSAL: GAI of $3,500, Federal tax: $1,756. KEEP: $14,744

Low-Wage Earner (approx. 61 percent of tax-filers make less than this)

$25,000 Income making $4,500 RRSP contribution
CURRENT: Federal tax and CPP/UI premiums: $3,561. KEEP: $21,439
PROPOSAL: Federal tax including surtaxes: $3,516. KEEP: $21,484

Medium-Wage Earner

$50,000 Income making $9,000 RRSP contribution
CURRENT: Federal tax and CPP/UI premiums: $8,827. KEEP: $41,173
PROPOSAL: Federal tax: $11,740. KEEP: $38,260

High-Wage Earner

$100,000 Income making $18,000 RRSP contribution
CURRENT: Federal tax and premiums: $20,681. KEEP: $79,319
PROPOSAL: Federal tax: $31,459. KEEP: $68,541

Student

Loans, summer minimum-wage job, $2,500 tuition
CURRENT: $5,280 loans and $4,334 earnings
CURRENT: KEEP $9,614. OWE: $5,280
PROPOSAL: Earn $4,334, GAI $7,833. KEEP: $11,360. OWE: $0

Notes

1. Unless stated otherwise, revenue and expenses are those found in the actual federal budget.

EIGHT

DEALING WITH AN ADOLESCENT CANADA

• • • • • • • • • •
CRAIG J. MACADAM

A resident of Lower Sackville, Nova Scotia, Craig is entering his second year in the Business Administration program at Bishop's University in Lennoxville, Quebec. Last year he won the Col. Arthur Mills Prize for Best All-Around First Year Student. A former member of the Nova Scotia alpine ski team, Craig skied for the Bishop's University team. He is a member of the Big Buddy Association, a Bishop's organization similar to the Big Brothers Association, and served as a "big buddy" to his friend Matthew, a student at one of the nearby elementary schools in Lennoxville, Quebec.

AS A SOCIETY, CANADA IS NOT RESPONSIBLE ENOUGH TO be left unattended. We will always need the guidance of our baby-sitter, the government. But like any growing child, there comes a time when we have to have some freedom to grow. It is time for the Canadian government to let its children, the citizens of Canada, have a bit more freedom.

As prime minister of Canada, I would initiate measures that would give Canadians and Canadian industry that freedom. These changes would include reforms to the organizational structure of our government. Amendments would have to be made to our social programs and laws to make Canada a more profitable environment for businesses of all sizes. And drastic changes in our education system would be necessary to support this more capitalist society.

Restructuring Our Government

The Canadian government must be restructured. There are too many instances in which rigid and bureaucratic government policies prevent Canadian businesses from being as profitable as their international competitors. Also, many of society's jobs are being carried out by an inefficient public sector when the profit-driven private sector could do them more efficiently and effectively, at a lower cost to our taxpayers.

We can no longer afford to use government as a vehicle to create jobs. Our government's sole purpose should be to manage our country. This would demand changes in its organizational structures. Rather than having ten very diverse provinces and two territories, the country could be more effectively and efficiently managed by a system with fewer regions, containing more equivalent amounts of land, natural resources, and populations.

I would propose six regions, roughly equivalent to our present-day Atlantic Provinces, Quebec, Southern Ontario, Northern Ontario and the Prairies, Western Alberta and British Columbia, and the Territories. This is a natural geographic division to which Canadians already relate because this is roughly how our natural resources and different industries are divided across the country.

This organizational structure would eliminate a lot of government duplication. More equivalent shares of our resources and population would make each area more economically independent and eventually eliminate the need for transfer payments from rich provinces to poor.

We would need leaders in this organizational structure that really understand economics and have the guts to act appropriately. We lose a lot of these people to business because the rewards are better. We should offer salaries and bonuses to our national leaders that would be comparable to what CEOs of large multinational corporations make. There are some experienced, great minds out there that should be recruited to help our country. Unfortunately, great minds do not come cheap.

Nurturing a Profitable Environment for Industry

We have to change the Canadian work ethic. In general, our people are less productive than their global competitors. We must motivate our less productive workers to be more productive. If they need help, we should provide it, but if they insist on being unproductive, they should be fired. An appropriate work ethic would be drilled into our workers during their education in the privately operated system I will propose below.

Government must take action to make these changes possible and affordable for Canadian business. This means abolishing minimum-wage laws, dissolving our unions, and ensuring that social assistance goes only to those who truly need it.

Minimum-wage laws are a cause of unemployment. With today's machines, an unskilled employee no longer produces enough output to justify paying him or her what our laws dictate. Therefore, a firm will replace the employee with a more cost-efficient machine. Minimum-wage laws do not let the market system work freely to determine an equilibrium in wage rates and unemployment levels. Canada does not have a supply of labour that is large enough to drive wage rates below a level that would be inhumane.

Without unions, corporations could make decisions a lot more quickly. Executives make decisions in the best interests of the share-holders. Canadian companies should be giving employees easier access to substantial shares in their companies so that executive decisions would also be in the best interests of the employees. Eliminating unions would allow workers and management to work together instead of against each other. Unions have outlived their usefulness in Canada. Our country has already evolved to the point at which we can act in a just and humane manner without union interference.

Welfare, unemployment insurance, and other social programs have a detrimental effect on the Canadian work ethic. They take from those who work and give to those who do not. This discourages our good employees from giving it their all. It takes away from the philosophy that urges us to strive, achieve, then get a just reward. If we take less from the achievers and give less to the underachievers, then more will strive to achieve, and the resultant output will supply more rewards.

In other words, the rich have proven that they are successful in making money. That is why they are rich. If government takes more of their income they will not bother to make so much. But if the government takes a smaller percentage of their pie, they will work harder to make more. Let the poor earn their incomes by working for the rich to help the rich get richer. When the rich are richer, there is a bigger pie to pay the salaries of the poor. If you take from the rich and give to the poor, then everybody just gets poorer.

Revamping Our Education System

With every new freedom there comes an added responsibility. If we are to unleash our citizens and let them live with less government intervention, we have to make sure that they have the knowledge to take care of themselves. Today's education system is not adequate to prepare our children to accept these new responsibilities.

Currently, each province manages its own education system. While every region should have its own courses to teach students about their particular region, we need a common core curriculum that is consistent throughout the country. We are all Canadians, from St. John's to Victoria to Tuktoyaktuk. If we are to act as a unified country, we should be taught as such.

The Canada-wide core curriculum would have to consist of subjects that teach students how to deal with the real world as it currently exists. Computer instruction and technology training are essential. At least one second language should be known by every Canadian if we are to succeed globally as international traders. Education about foreign cultures should be added to our textbooks. Of course, the traditional subjects will always be important.

Today, economics is a very important field, a field in which we have failed to educate our citizens. In so doing, we are making economic growth harder than it has to be. Economics is a topic that should be taught to children like arithmetic. We must find creative ways to make it a learner-friendly subject so that the workings of our economic system become common sense. If we are willing to let our people run the country democratically, we must teach them how investment, interest rates, inflation, currency exchange, and other economic processes really work. For this reason, economics should be a part of the core curriculum.

We should have a federal governing body to monitor the core curriculum program. Standard evaluation exams should be administered across the country to see which areas have problems. Beyond that, we should transfer our educational responsibilities to the private sector to administer an education that tends to each region's industrial needs. For example, students in Saskatchewan would be taught about agriculture by representatives from the wheat industry, while children in Labrador would learn how ore deposits are extracted from the earth by mining industry representatives. The private sector will be hiring our children in the future, so they should be playing a role in educating them. Ongoing productive interaction between school administration, students, parents, and the private sector is the key to determining exactly what our education system needs and how to get it.

I would strive to have our educational system eventually evolve to the point where schools would be run as profit-making educational firms. Competition between education firms would enhance the quality of the education that Canadians receive. The profit motive would encourage innovative entrepreneurs to find ways to provide every child with an educational environment that best suits his or her needs.

Corporations would pay post-secondary education firms for their trained students upon graduation. Post-secondary firms would pay secondary firms for their graduates. This flow of revenue would filter down to the pre-elementary level, with each education firm preparing its students for the next level. Each firm's existence would be dependent upon its ability to provide quality education, because every education firm could simply purchase its incoming students from a better competitor if its current feeder schools let it down.

This system would induce profit incentives for education managers. It would force managers to attend to problems where today's education system fails. In most cases today, when a problem is not solved by the last bell, it is no longer the teacher's problem. In a profit-making system, an education manager would not be able to afford to leave problems unsolved.

Rather than having corporations pay taxes into a kitty to pay for all of society's needs, we must determine who benefits from our education system and have those beneficiaries pay for what they need directly. In today's system, too much is lost in bureaucratic waste and the lack of economic accountability that the public sector has in running our schools. If businesses pay their taxes as fees directly to our education firms, we see exactly what we are getting for our money. Education managers would strive to offer a quality product — in this case, educated students. Corporations would look to get these products at the best price, therefore putting pressure on the education managers to use their funds wisely and provide these products cost-efficiently.

As prime minister, I would also implement a program to make it mandatory for all students to take a year off between secondary and post-secondary education to travel across the country. Such a program could be run cost-effectively if it were done with economies of scale. Private industry could help fund the program in return for labour that the students would supply during this year. Consequently, Canadian industry would have access to a more competent labour force once each student completed his or her education. Students would complete their education with an appreciation for the entire country, not just their own backyards. They would also have had a taste of the real world.

Unity

Unifying the country is not something in the prime minister's direct control. Unity is a state of mind that must be instilled in our citizens through indirect means. My proposal to decentralize government does not have to push the regions apart. Through mutually beneficial trade, our regions would be closely linked. Through a student exchange program, Canadians would develop friendships across the country. A stronger work ethic, created by the elimination of social policies, would make our citizens proud to be Canadians. As prime minister, I would do my best to provide an economically prosperous environment to dispel the hate and distrust that often prevail during hard economic times.

The Quebec question is a problem that must be solved soon. The uncertainty around Quebec's situation keeps the Canadian dollar under-valued and interest rates high. High interest rates discourage Canadians and Canadian firms from making investment expenditures that we must make if our economy is going to grow. Canada will always have high interest rates until Quebec comes to a decision. Until that decision is made, all of Canada, including Quebec, will suffer.

I think Quebec is fighting for something that the rest of Canada should be fighting for. We must restructure government in such a way that the regions of Canada are given more freedom to act in pursuit of their own best interests. Quebec is fighting for this right. The six regions I have proposed should each be fighting for this right. Decentralization and empowerment work for large multinationals, and these principles should also be applied to the government's management of a country. I say, give Quebec what it wants, and give it to the other regions of Canada, too!

Standard of Living

Living standards and quality of life are hard things to measure. The changes I have proposed might not improve the quality of life for every Canadian, but I feel they would make life better for those who are willing to work. Less government means fewer taxes, but it also means fewer social services for those who do not pull their weight. Profit-driven schools would not be a place for lazy students. Eliminating unions and other socialist policies would not make life easier for the unproductive worker. However, I believe that the changes I have proposed take away the option of a free ride. They will force every Canadian to put forth an effort to make Canada grow economically. When we are strong economically, then we can all enjoy a better quality of life.

Lighting the Fire

Canada is due for a pep talk. I think the prime minister should get up in front of all Canadians and make a memorable performance to light a fire under Canadian patriotism. I am thinking of the whole nine yards: all television and radio stations tuned in, podium speech, arms flailing, fists pounding, and a script to go down in the history books. The entire country would stop for ten minutes and listen.

The content would have to be new and fresh, enough to ignite a big change. It would be a message to every Canadian about what it means to be Canadian today, not yesterday. It would announce to the rest of the world, "Look out, because here we come!" It would have to get us moving, and it would have to be powerful enough to keep us moving for ten, twenty, and fifty years. We need something to remember and we need something to believe in … we need a hero!

We must call on every Canadian to make short-term sacrifices if we are to make Canada the greatest country it has the potential to be. Hundreds of thousands of Canadians have made the ultimate sacrifice by giving their lives in past wars, fighting for the rights we have today. I think we owe it to those individuals to make some little sacrifices of our own.

These are my suggestions.

Perhaps someday, if we can all agree on a right way to do things, Canadians will never have to make any more sacrifices.

NINE

UN PLAN PERSONNEL, FAMILIAL, ET SOCIAL

• • • • • • • • • •
BENOIT POIRIER

A native of Vaudreuil, Quebec, Benoit is entering a Ph.D. program in engineering at the University of Montreal. He is a reserve member of the Canadian Armed Forces and served as a UN peacekeeping officer both in Cyprus and at the scene of the Oka crisis. He is also president of his own business, Innovations PI 4 Inc., which manufactures new plastic injections moulded products. Benoit is a volunteer organizer for the Terry Fox Run and a member of Montreal's Junior Chamber of Commerce.

CE DOCUMENT SE VEUT UNE RÉFLEXION SUR LE NIVEAU DE vie et sur l'unité nationale. Comment permettre à un Canadien[1] de se développer au niveau personnel, familial, et social tout en favorisant l'unité canadienne? Actuellement, les structures en place privilégient le travailleur nanti tout en défavorisant les jeunes (diplômés ou non), les personnes âgées, les immigrants, les autochtones, les défavorisés sociaux, les malades, etc. Dans une société libérale comme la nôtre, il est primordial de réfléchir sur le rôle du gouvernement comme vecteur de ressources … Trois plans complémentaires sont proposés: plan personnel, plan familial et plan social. Certaines des idées suggérées relèvent du domaine provincial. Par conséquent, un premier ministre canadien pourra certainement influencer ses homologues provinciaux.

Plan Personnel
À la veille du nouveau millénaire, on ne peut pas passer sous silence les trop nombreux Canadiens qui ne peuvent subvenir à leur besoins

essentiels de base (p. ex., familles sous le seuil de la pauvreté, itinérants, etc.). Le plan personnel se compose donc de trois volets majeurs.

Volet santé

Chaque individu a droit à un minimum de confort: logement, nourriture, vêtement et amour. Une vie équilibrée permet à l'individu de s'épanouir. L'espoir, les rêves sont alors possibles permettant ainsi de se projeter dans l'avenir. La santé est un élément essentiel de cet épanouissement. Des moyens seront présentés plus loin dans le texte.

Un billet modérateur est nécessaire pour l'assurance maladie, puisqu'on retrouve trop d'abus dans le système. Le système actuel de santé devrait se nommer "système de maladie." Les médecins soignent les malades. La prévention est un concept sous utilisé. L'innovation est de former des spécialistes de la santé (et non des médecins). Ces spécialistes insisteraient sur la prévention pour maintenir la santé physique, psychologique et sexuelle en plus d'encourager les exercices physiques ainsi qu'une alimentation saine et équilibrée.

Volet éducation

Le système d'éducation proposé possède trois niveaux. Les personnes avec difficultés d'apprentissage sont regroupées ensemble. Le système s'applique à la majorité des étudiants en y apportant toutefois certaines modifications, telles que l'encouragement à assister aux périodes d'études supervisées. Les personnes douées ou ayant des capacités supérieures, quant à elles, sont encouragées à participer à un programme accéléré. De meilleurs mécanismes pour le développement de l'étudiant seront disponibles. Par exemple, les cours se donneraient sur quatre jours; des activités complémentaires se donneraient le cinquième jour. Ces étudiants doués deviendront probablement les futurs entrepreneurs, professionnels, et leaders de demain.

Plusieurs aspects sont importants dans le développement des individus. Il faut, entre autres, insister sur le goût de s'instruire, d'apprendre et surtout de développer. L'exploration de différentes activités, telles que le sport, la danse, la musique, le théâtre et autres, pourra s'intégrer facilement à la découverte de différentes régions de son pays grâce à divers concours. Au Québec, les compétitions inter-universitaires sont rares. Par exemple, aucune équipe de football ou de hockey ne représente l'Université de Montréal. La compétition et la rivalité permettent le développement de liens entre les étudiants et les universités en plus de les familiariser avec diverses régions.

Les concours permettent de développer l'imagination et la créativité. Une meilleure publicité au sujet des concours, tout en offrant d'intéressants prix, inciterait les jeunes à participer. L'implication des entreprises, ainsi que leur soutien lors de concours d'envergure, permettrait aux jeunes Canadiens de se regrouper nationalement selon un intérêt commun tout en représentant leur région.

La jeunesse d'aujourd'hui pourra, tout en s'amusant et grâce à certains outils disponibles, découvrir le Canada. Le "crayon" de l'avenir est maintenant le puissant ordinateur (Internet). Les jeunes ont la chance d'utiliser des outils puissants pour voyager à travers le monde et/ou le pays rapidement. En effet, avec l'avènement de la technologie, il sera facile de regrouper différentes écoles à travers le pays et de favoriser des liens d'échanges et d'amitiés. En plus d'établir des liens, les étudiants des diverses régions pourront se regrouper pour effectuer des travaux d'histoire ou de géographie. Le Canadien est présentement ignorant de ce que son voisin (autre province) peut offrir. Le goût de voyager et de visiter une région inconnue du Canada sera beaucoup plus facile à satisfaire grâce à l'autoroute électronique. Ce mur franchi pourra, par la suite, amener les parents à se côtoyer et, peut-être, à devenir amis.

L'école doit valoriser et favoriser autant les études universitaires que techniques puisque la société a besoin de tous ces différents spécialistes. Il faut préconiser les études et les stages de façon à développer le goût de ce que l'étudiant fera pendant une importante partie de sa vie. Les compagnies pourraient investir en encourageant le développement des étudiants de tous les niveaux dès le secondaire, en offrant notamment des stages. L'intégration de l'industrie (p. ex., métier, spécialité) au milieu des études est nécessaire pour permettre aux étudiants d'être performants dans ce monde où la distance n'a plus d'importance.

Volet emploi

La société moderne oblige la majorité des hommes à travailler. Une législation éliminerait le temps supplémentaire en obligeant les employés à travailler des semaines de quatre jours, leur laissant ainsi une journée de plus pour leurs loisirs. Des emplois seraient ainsi automatiquement créés. Certains aspects sont essentiels au développement et à la survie de notre société:

- Encourager la créativité, l'imagination, et l'initiative locale des PME;
- Effectuer une meilleure gestion des ressources naturelles (planification, rationalisation, nettoyage, protection, recyclage, élevage, reboisement, etc.);
- Valoriser le rôle de chacun dans l'équilibre écologique;
- Développer des liens entre les entreprises et les universités dans le domaine des hautes technologies.

La recherche et le développement (R&D) permettent aux compagnies de survivre et de rester leader dans leur domaine. De meilleurs programmes devraient encourager les compagnies à investir dans la R&D. Des programmes de subvention pour les jeunes entreprises en collaboration (supervision) avec les universités seraient proposés. Ces jeunes pleins d'idées n'ont pas souvent les moyens de s'aventurer. Enfin, il est primordial que les petites compagnies existantes modifient leur façon d'opérer et s'adaptent aux nouveaux moyens (c.-à-d. informatique, télécommunication et environnement) afin de devenir plus compétitives et plus efficaces. Nous sommes dans une nouvelle ère où la compétition est féroce et les frontières n'existent plus. Nos anciens compétiteurs de la ville voisine devront devenir rapidement nos meilleurs alliés pour survivre à l'envahisseur étranger (p. ex., américain, européen, asiatique).

Plan Familial

Nous sommes toujours pressés, le temps nous manque. Les jeunes souffrent de l'absence de leurs parents. Ceux-ci confient trop souvent l'éducation de leurs enfants à l'école où il est difficile, lors de l'adolescence, d'inculquer aux jeunes le respect de soi et des autres. L'absence de la maison des parents est une source de démotivation nuisible au développement des jeunes. Les parents doivent assumer leurs responsabilités en tant que parents en développant les valeurs familiales. La semaine de quatre jours, difficile à accepter au début (salaire moindre), favorisera le développement de la famille et des loisirs. Les parents auront plus de temps pour organiser leur vie familiale, d'éduquer leurs enfants et partager des loisirs communs. Notons que la société nécessitera beaucoup plus spécialistes en loisir. Étant au travail, les parents devraient avoir un accès facile aux garderies. Par ailleurs, les aînés vivent une terrible solitude. Il faut valoriser les activités des aînés. Leur expérience et leur dévouement pourraient s'utiliser plus favorablement. Pourquoi ne pas intégrer un système de garderie avec la présence des personnes âgées? Pourquoi ne pas utiliser leurs compétences pour aider tous ceux et celles qui en auraient besoin?

Plan Social

Il est important d'inculquer différentes valeurs aux jeunes malgré le déchirement de plusieurs familles. Les jeunes ont besoin de s'identifier à quelqu'un, d'appartenir à un groupe. Des modèles aident les jeunes dans leur développement. C'est ici que le milieu parascolaire jouera un rôle beaucoup plus important. Les activités parascolaires devraient être offertes par l'école ou les centres communautaires. Les activités enseignées, soit le soir ou la fin de semaine, correspondent à un besoin de la société actuelle puisque les parents (en couple ou seul) vivent selon des horaires contraignants et variés. Des activités contrôlées et supervisées, telles que les cadets, les scouts, les clubs de hockey, les groupes de théâtre, les comités d'environnement ou d'informatique, empêchent le jeune de s'ennuyer ou de penser à des mauvais tours. Elles permettent d'éduquer les jeunes dans divers domaines. Les problèmes reliés à la drogue ou à la délinquance peuvent ainsi diminuer. La participation à l'école d'un sport ou d'une activité valorisante pour l'élève va créer un lien d'appartenance, de motivation et sera un atout de plus pour éviter le décrochage.

Pour permettre à tous les jeunes de vivre des expériences de travail, on devrait offrir divers programmes d'emploi (p. ex., armée, garde côtière, environnement, aide aux malades ou personnes âgées, etc.). Chacun devrait s'inscrire à un de ces programmes durant ses études sous forme de stage estival. Quant aux décrocheurs, ils devront être encadrés par un de ces organismes jusqu'à ce qu'ils obtiennent une formation de base pour gagner leur vie.

La population en générale est irresponsable. On veut que le gouvernement fournisse tous les services gratuitement, spécialement celui de créer notre emploi. Malheureusement, nous aurons toujours du monde qui aura besoin de l'aide de la société. Un comité évaluerait les demandes d'aide sociale. Un regroupement de ressources permettrait à ces personnes de pouvoir se prendre en main. Différents professionnels pourraient gérer ces ressources et les aider à apprendre un nouveau métier afin de pouvoir se débrouiller. Par exemple, un lieu commun regroupant plusieurs familles (p. ex., base militaire désaffectée) où différents services supervisés seraient disponibles (p. ex., cafétéria, magasin de linge, garderie). Ces services seraient assurés par les bénéficiaires. En plus de recevoir une formation, ils devront (ceux dont la santé le permettent) effectuer des tâches (p. ex., cuisine, nettoyage, visite des malades ou des personnes âgées, aide aux handicapés, nettoyage de l'environnement, reboisement, etc.). Ces bonnes causes aideront sûrement à développer des qualités de partage, d'amitié, d'honnêteté et de fierté. La solution étant souvent associée au problème, leur implication dans ces divers projets sera sûrement une source de motivation pour les aider à se prendre en main. Dans une même ligne d'idée, l'assurance-chômage serait aussi modifiée. Une grande majorité de gens tirent profit de ce système en tardant souvent à se trouver un emploi. Ils devront se chercher un emploi, se former ou bien faire du bénévolat.

Le peuple autochtone ainsi que les immigrants sont souvent mis à l'écart. Le goût d'aider les autres pourrait s'amalgamer à l'intégration des nouveaux émigrés ainsi que des peuples autochtones à travers les centres communautaires. L'aide présentement donnée aux autochtones est mal gérée puisque l'argent qu'ils reçoivent nuit à la formation des jeunes. Leur formation est essentielle à la survie de leur peuple puisque la richesse d'une personne est mesurée par la connaissance acquise. Ils s'enfoncent dans la décadence (c.-à-d., drogues, alcool, inceste). Il faut les intégrer et les impliquer dans des projets communs afin qu'ils puissent avoir un sens d'appartenance à un groupe et se sentir fiers d'être canadiens.

Des projets devraient favoriser le développement de l'individu et de sa communauté en impliquant tous les citoyens (p. ex., jeunes, handicapés, prisonniers, etc.). Une bonne connaissance de leur milieu permet de réunir les gens. Ils peuvent ainsi partager ces connaissances avec différentes régions. Cette richesse est partagée de façon à lier les différents groupes. Ces projets pourront réunir les aspects économiques, sociaux, et politiques. Les centres communautaires posséderont les humaines pour imaginer ces projets. Si ces projets viennent de la communauté, il sera beaucoup plus facile d'inciter les individus à y participer. Une position commune, un but commun pourraient réunir les différentes régions du Canada. Les centres communautaires permettront de favoriser les échanges entre les individus. Les gens pourront se rassembler afin de trouver une identité propre au peuple multiculturel canadien. Nous devrons nous trouver une identité afin de nous démarquer des Américains dont nous dépendons trop souvent.

Avec la globalisation des marchés, le Canada est un pays trop grand pour le nombre limité de ses citoyens. L'appareil gouvernemental existant est beaucoup trop onéreux. Ce territoire ne devrait contenir que cinq régions (Maritimes, Québec, Ontario, Prairies et Pacifique). Une décentralisation des pouvoirs devrait s'effectuer en diminuant le recoupement des opérations. Au Québec, par exemple, il y a des ministères fédéraux et des ministères provinciaux du Revenu, de la Justice, des Transports, des Communications, de l'Environnement, des polices fédérale, provinciale et municipale. C'est bureaucratique, trop dispendieux, et inefficace. Le gouvernement fédéral, tout comme les gouvernements provinciaux, devraient diminuer de beaucoup le nombre de leurs députés. Ceux-ci s'occuperaient d'un plus grand territoire en utilisant leurs adjoints. L'abolition du poste de gouverneur général et la modification de l'onéreux Sénat seraient des priorités. Le Sénat ressemblerait à un comité d'administration d'une grande entreprise qui est habituellement composé de quelques membres. Enfin, plusieurs ministères nécessitent des changements afin de s'adapter à la nouvelle réalité de l'an 2000 (p. ex., Justice, Défense nationale). Peut-être verrons-nous l'apparition de l'argent électronique?

Nos anciens élus ont pris souvent de mauvaises décisions qui sont présentement nuisibles au développement économique du Canada. Il est inconcevable que nos grands-parents, nos parents, nous les jeunes et nos enfants payent durant toute une vie la note due à ces mauvaises décisions. Pourquoi ces élus reçoivent-ils une généreuse pension? Pour leurs erreurs? Le système de pension des parlementaires ainsi que celui des fonctionnaires (incluant les généreuses primes) devrait être complètement modifié. Par ailleurs, un professionnel (p. ex., ingénieur, médecin, dentiste, avocat) reçoit une formation pour bien performer dans sa profession. Pourquoi n'importe qui peut devenir ministre? L'école de la vie permet-elle à un individu d'acquérir les capacités à mener un ministère ou un état? Ceci est à l'encontre de la philosophie des universités, et des grandes entreprises.

Ayant travaillé pour le ministère de la Défense, je sais que l'appareil bureaucratique gouvernemental existant est beaucoup trop lourd et inefficace. Les fonctionnaires dirigent des projets dont ils dépensent inutilement, et souvent inconsciemment, d'importantes sommes des fonds publics. Une nouvelle façon de travailler en assujettissant le fonctionnaire aux conséquences de ses actes serait nécessaire. Les députés, par exemple, assumeraient la responsabilité de leurs erreurs par leur démission obligatoire avec pénalité monétaire.

Conclusion

Beaucoup de travail reste à faire pour éliminer notre dette, pour diminuer le crime organisé, pour harmoniser les différentes communautés. Beaucoup de pays envient le nôtre où justice, paix, et liberté règnent. Le nouveau millénaire devrait donner un pays où la Reine serait remplacée par un nouveau terme où tous les Canadiens s'identifieront. Il faut changer la mentalité des citoyens: "l'État doit TOUT me fournir." Ne devrions-nous pas adapter la célèbre phrase du président Kennedy: "Ne demandez pas ce que le Canada peut faire pour vous, mais ce que vous pouvez faire pour le Canada?" Le jeune, qui deviendra le citoyen de demain, aura une grande responsabilité. Il connaîtra probablement mieux notre pays grâce, notamment, à l'autoroute électronique. Il sera donc en mesure de vanter toutes les qualités qui se rattachent à notre beau pays, le Canada, et d'en être fier.

Notes

1. Sens générique du mot à travers le document.

TEN

THE FUTURE OF CANADA: RESPONDING TO THE CHALLENGE TODAY

• • • • • • • • • •
KAREN HAMILTON

After majoring in Political Science at St. Thomas University, Karen is now enrolled in the Faculty of Law at the University of New Brunswick in Fredericton. At St. Thomas University, Karen was a member of the debating society, a member of the university choir, and president of the Political Science Society. She also played the lead role in a campus production of Edward Albee's The Sandbox. *Karen served as the student representative on a number of departmental committees and was a founding member of the Pre-Law Society at St. Thomas University.*

HOW DOES ONE DEFINE CANADA? IS CANADA A PRODUCT of the marriage between two founding nations, a partnership between provinces or regions, or simply the homeland of twenty-seven million citizens?

Canada may be defined in a variety of ways, but these different interpretations tend to contradict each other and complicate the government's job. Fundamental divisions exist within our political community and have become increasingly difficult to bridge. To compound the problem, Canadians are seeing the erosion of their earning and spending powers and are becoming more vocal in their dissatisfaction with government. Today the prime minister is faced with an enormous set of challenges. On the one hand, Canadians must be persuaded that their particular needs and aspirations can best be met within a unified Canada. On the other hand, if Canadians are to maintain present living standards with any hope of future improvement, the prime minister must make tough economic decisions that will likely be politically unpopular. These are daunting tasks that must be undertaken if Canada is to survive. As prime minister, I would have three top priorities: to reach out to Quebec, to address western discontent, and to demand that Canada become fiscally responsible.

The greatest threat to Canada's continued viability is the upcoming Quebec referendum on sovereignty. Although Canadians may be tired of Quebec's ongoing threats and demands, the time is not right to be complacent. With both Parizeau and Bouchard intent on dismantling Canada, the rest of the country should be asking some very important questions. If Quebec separates, would the remaining provinces be capable of uniting in some restructured form, or would the pull from our southern neighbour be too strong? Without Quebec, would Canada inevitably become part of the United States? Are Canadians prepared to gamble that assimilation would not occur if Quebec does leave?

If Canadians are determined to remain independent from the United States, then Canada, including Quebec, must be strongly united. According to Alexander Brady, two key factors make Canada different from the United States: our French–English component and our parliamentary system of government.[1] As Brady argues, these factors alone are sufficient justification to keep the two countries separate. But could our parliamentary system of government not be changed? It might be a formidable undertaking, but it's a possible one, by way of constitutional amendment. And the fundamental bilingual and bicultural aspect of Canada exists only because both English-speaking and French-speaking people make Canada their home. If Quebec separates, this uniqueness would be virtually eliminated. As Brady argues, the threat of Canada's absorption by the United States can only be counterbalanced by a strong, united Canada that includes Quebec.

This author accepts Brady's theory that the key to keeping Canada separate from the United States is to keep Quebec within Canada. But what can the prime minister do to reach out to Quebeckers without alienating the rest of the country? How can the prime minister make Quebeckers feel they are truly a part of Canada when both the Meech Lake and Charlottetown Accords failed to do just that?

The status quo is obviously no longer an acceptable alternative. The separatist movement in Quebec is proof enough. But another round of constitutional talks is not the answer either. As Peter Russell argues, after more than thirty years of wrangling, constitutional fatigue has stricken the Canadian public.[2] However, to forgo what Russell calls "mega constitutional politics" in the foreseeable future does not mean that the prime minister is precluded from implementing some changes to Canada's political framework. Changes that might work towards strengthening and unifying Canada could be undertaken now, without resorting to constitutional amendment.

Quebec separatists have argued that remaining in Canada prevents them from becoming "masters in their own house." They charge the national government with encroachment in areas of provincial jurisdiction, thus interfering with Quebec's ability to preserve its distinctness.[3]

It is doubtful whether Quebec would ever have agreed to unite with the other three provinces in Confederation without a guarantee of federalism. At that time, the provincial governments were established to ensure that cultural matters and local issues, which were of primary concern to Quebec, would be handled at the provincial level. The national government was to focus mainly on managing the economy, promoting nation-building, and providing security for the developing country. Sections 91 and 92 of the British North America Act, 1867, outlined the responsibilities of the two levels of government. However, by the 1920s the division between the two jurisdictions had become blurred.

As Donald Smiley points out, the national government, in response to demands from English Canada, became more active in areas that had previously been administered solely by the provinces.[4] An attitude prevailed in English Canada that certain crucial political objectives could be achieved only through national government action. Issues such as the protection of Canadian culture from American encroachment and the establishment of broad national standards in social policy resulted in more and more overlap between sections 91 and 92. The terms of the original deal that brought Quebec into Confederation were slowly being eroded. As intervention by Ottawa increased, so did Quebec's dissatisfaction.

In order to satisfy Quebec, the division of powers must once again become clearly defined. In Quebec's case, a return must be made to the original agreement of 1867. This action might not be enough to satisfy the separatists, but it would signal Ottawa's willingness to give serious consideration to Quebeckers and their aspirations. Such a "reaching out" might be enough to ensure that separatists are unable to increase their level of support within Quebec, thus lessening their chances of winning the upcoming referendum.

A return to the original terms of 1867 might be agreeable to Quebec but might not be welcomed by the rest of the country. However, does the division of powers between Quebec and Ottawa necessarily have to be the same as that between other provinces and Ottawa? As long as there are no changes to the responsibilities actually listed in sections 91 and 92, could the provinces not negotiate individually with Ottawa as to how much overlap they each want? As Smiley argues, a system of asymmetrical federalism has the potential to satisfy Quebec's demands for less intervention from Ottawa and an English Canada that might still favour a strong central government.

There may be other ways of placating those provinces opposed to a so-called special treatment deal for Quebec (although I would argue that asymmetrical federalism is not a special deal for Quebec because the option would be open to other provinces as well). Traditionally, the western provinces have complained of less-than-equal treatment in their dealings with central Canada. From feelings of alienation stemming from not being original partners in Confederation, to complaints regarding tariffs, freight rates, and the terms of the National Energy Policy, the West has developed a grievance mentality. The belief that Confederation is no longer a good deal for the West is reflected in the size of the protest vote cast in the most recent federal election. At times, the traditional national parties have been shut out completely in parts of the West.

Although "western separation" does not appear to pose as realistic a threat to Canada as Quebec separation does, the prime minister has the means to, and therefore should, address some of these regional concerns. Over 80 percent of westerners believe the West is ignored because the national political parties receive most of their votes from Ontario and Quebec.[5] The West's biggest complaint is the lack of adequate representation in Parliament.

Both the Meech Lake and Charlottetown Accords proposed changes to the method of Senate selection in response to western demands. A Triple-E Senate (Equal, Elected, Effective) is the ultimate goal of the

West, but it would be impossible to achieve without constitutional amendment. Nevertheless, the prime minister has the means of satisfying a portion of the West's Senate aspirations right now. When a vacancy occurs, Senate appointments could be filled through provincial nominations, or even by provincial elections. The West might feel less alienated if it exercised more control over who is sent to Ottawa to represent regional concerns. This may be a symbolic gesture more than anything, because Senate seat distribution would not change. However, giving the provinces control over Senate appointments would certainly be a sign of good faith and an indication that the prime minister is concerned with more than just satisfying Quebec.

In addition to reaching out to Quebec and addressing western grievances, the prime minister must unequivocally promote fiscal responsibility. The goal of unifying Canada cannot be separated from economic goals. If Canada is prosperous, investments will be made, jobs will be created, economic opportunities will abound, and living standards will improve. With more people working and paying taxes, more money will be available for the less fortunate and for the national social programs Canadians hold so dear. With prosperity comes pride. If Canadians live in a country with a robust, healthy economy, a land of opportunity, they will be less inclined to want to dismantle that same country or to live somewhere else. A prosperous Canada is more likely to be a united Canada.

Paul Martin's recent budget points Canada in the right fiscal direction but simply does not go far enough. Canada is sinking fast under a tremendous debt load, which is growing at an alarming rate. The recent downgrading of Canada's triple-A bond rating should be sufficient to convince the government that decisive action must be taken without further delay. If Canada is to have a future at all, especially one controlled by Canadians rather than by foreign debt-holders, painful and unpopular decisions can no longer be put off.

According to statistics recently cited in *The Globe and Mail*, Mr. Martin proposes to reduce the deficit to $32.7 billion in 1995–96 and $24.3 billion in 1996–97.[6] Supporters applaud Martin for successfully reducing the deficit, albeit on paper, from its present $37.9 billion level. But what supporters seem to overlook is the fact that Mr. Martin's reduced deficit figures will still add $57 billion to the debt over the next two years.

Canada's current debt stands at almost $550 billion and is expected to reach $800 billion within five years, simply because of compound interest.[7] The interest payments on this massive debt consume close to one-third of all tax dollars every year. In addition to the federal debt, provincial debts and the future liabilities of the Canada and Quebec Pension Plans will have to be dealt with at some point. Inevitably, Canadians will be facing higher tax rates and shrinking pay cheques as interest payments increase in the future. Yet the federal government still does not respond as though Canada is facing a serious economic crisis.

As prime minister, I would insist that the deficit be reduced to zero within a maximum of three years, through spending cuts and not through tax increases. A plan would also be formulated to pay down the debt to a manageable level once the deficit had been eliminated. Lower personal and corporate tax rates would be phased in to promote investment, savings, the creation of jobs, and to put more money back in the pockets of working Canadians. Higher tax rates mean that individual Canadians are less and less able to look after themselves and their families. Terence Corcoran in *The Globe and Mail* recently commented on "the establishment view of Canada as a nation of welfare-state sheep who need to be herded by layers of bureaucrats and politicians."[8] But Canadians can no longer afford to support a system of expensive, paternalistic government. It is time to promote personal responsibility and accountability. As tax rates are lowered, Canadians must be educated and encouraged to spend their own money on their own well-being.

Balancing the budget while also providing tax reductions will involve massive expenditure cuts. When deciding where to make cuts, everything must be on the table for consideration; nothing can be untouchable. It is time to stop saddling future generations with our present excesses. To start with, the federal civil service must be drastically reduced. While Canada's population tripled between 1910 and 1984, the federal civil service increased from 20,000 to 250,000 over the same period.[9] All crown corporations must also be examined. If a corporation can be operated more efficiently and economically in the private sector, then it must be sold.

Universality of social programs is no longer a viable expectation. Social programs must be targeted specifically at those Canadians truly in need. Otherwise, all Canadians will have to shoulder the increasingly crippling expenses. Consider the Canada Pension Plan, for example. Peter Taylor comments that the present 5.4 percent payroll deduction is estimated to reach a punitive 14–16 percent by 2030.[10] But, as Taylor argues, retirement funding should be a "personal responsibility" rather than a "social obligation." To initially ease the drain on the public purse, the retirement age could be gradually increased. To encourage personal responsibility for retirement planning, registered retirement savings plan contribution limits and conditions could be made less restrictive.

As the size of government is decreased and services are cut, creative ideas can be implemented to ensure the most needy citizens are not abandoned. If Canadians are able to take home more of what they earn, they may likely be more generous with their charitable donations. To encourage community spirit, tax credits could be issued not only for cash donations but also for time volunteered to charitable organizations.

Unfortunately some people will experience hardship as expenditures are cut and Canadians learn not to rely on government as a cradle-to-grave provider. However, inconvenience and disruption must be faced today because the future of the country is at stake. Individual citizens can be encouraged to participate actively in the process as Canada becomes more fiscally responsible. Any cost-saving suggestions that are submitted and subsequently implemented could be rewarded with a tax credit.

If Canada does not get her fiscal house in order, Canadians will experience diminishing living standards and will be less able to care for the truly needy in the years ahead. Any short-term suffering will be more than offset if Canada can be preserved for our children without a legacy of debt.

There are no easy answers when considering how to unify Canada and improve living standards. Canada is faced with perennial problems, and more loom on the horizon. Political scholars such as George Grant and Goldwyn Smith argue that Canada inevitably will be assimilated by the United States. Canadians can either accept that argument and slip into complacency or attempt to prove them both wrong. Just because there are no *simple* solutions does not mean that solutions do not exist. It is important to remember that Canada has succeeded for almost 130 years. By exercising political will and determination today, the prime minister has the opportunity to lead Canadians into the twenty-first century within a united, prosperous country.

Notes

1. Alexander Brady, "The Meaning of Canadian Nationalism," *International Journal* 19, no. 2 (Summer 1964), pp. 348–63.
2. Peter H. Russell, *Constitutional Odyssey*, 2nd edition (Toronto: University of Toronto Press), pp. 228–9.
3. Marcel Côté and David Johnston, *If Quebec Goes ...* (Toronto: Stoddart, 1995).
4. Donald Smiley, "The Two Themes of Canadian Federalism," *The Canadian Political Tradition*, 2nd edition, R. S. Blair and J. T. McLeod, eds. (Scarborough: Nelson Canada, 1993), p. 49.
5. Roger Gibbons, *Conflict and Unity*, 2nd edition (Scarborough: Nelson Canada, 1990), p. 128.
6. *The Globe and Mail*, Tuesday, October 18, 1994, A1.
7. Ibid, A6.
8. *The Globe and Mail*, Wednesday, June 14, 1995, B2.
9. William Gairdner, *The Trouble with Canada* (Toronto: Stoddart, 1990), p. 103.
10. Peter Shawn Taylor, "Grandma! Grandpa! Back to Work!" *Saturday Night*, June 1995, p. 22.

ELEVEN

THE TROUBLE WITH CANADA AND HOW TO FIX IT

• • • • • • • • • •
WILLIAM D. GAIRDNER

*O*ne of Canada's most controversial social commentators, William Gairdner is an author, businessman, and former Olympic athlete. He is the former president and owner of The Fitness Institute, an organization providing professional fitness and lifestyle management services, and he competed for Canada in the decathlon at the 1964 Olympic Games. He also competed at the Pan American and Commonwealth Games, and is the former Canadian national champion in the 400-metre and 110-metre hurdles. William Gairdner holds a doctorate in English Literature from Stanford University. He is the author of two national bestsellers,* The Trouble with Canada *and* War against the Family.

THE QUESTION, "IF YOU WERE THE PRIME MINISTER OF Canada, what would you do to improve the living standard and unify the country?" is audacious, even incendiary. Dropped at any social gathering it is certain to excite everyone, from simpletons to distracted visionaries. The former are unaware of the concrete difficulties; the latter dismiss them. And the normal person between these extremes knows that trying to bring meaningful political harmony to Canada is like trying to melt an iceberg with a blow-torch, or steer an ocean liner with a toothpick.

Notice I said "harmony," not "change." Canada has too much change already, and the people are uneasy, frightened that we may be wandering like feverish lemmings into dangerous waters. And anyway, change for misguided purposes is just the beginning of chaos. Canada needs harmony, not change. To get harmony, it needs coherent and workable principles and ideals.

However, as a people, we labour under conflicting and increasingly incoherent political, economic, and social policies that seem to be hardening in a sclerotic gridlock everywhere we turn. Such gridlock can only be broken by a thorough, profound alteration in our fundamental institutions and values, root and branch. This requires not change so much as repudiation of our errors, and a return to foundational values and core beliefs.

Political philosophers from Plato to Tocqueville have warned us keenly that the warring interests and headlong pursuit of merely individual ends, so common to democracies, end in chaos, and then tyranny. That social breakdown is natural to democracy, fragmenting society in such a way that citizens begin to feel alienated — in fact, begin to feel, as Arnold Toynbee put it, that they are "in" but not "of" their society.

So, as your prime-minister-to-be, I wish to speak not about revolution, or social change, or about theory, but about what we can actually do to recover ourselves as a people. About how a conscious effort by a courageous people — first to recapture and vivify their traditional values, then to deliberately align their political and social institutions with those values in a single and coherent vision of positive political, economic, and social action — will surely bring harmony to Canada and prove these sceptical philosophers wrong.

The Political Solutions

A. J. P. Taylor once said something that is true of every free society; namely, that "until August, 1914, a sensible, law-abiding person could pass through life and hardly notice the existence of the state, beyond the local post office, and the policeman."

Well, how far we have departed from this refreshing condition! Canada — a nearly solvent nation in 1967, with a mere $20-billion cumulative debt from its entire first one hundred years of existence — is today by population smaller than the state of California, and yet has one of the worst per capita debts of any nation in the history of the world: well over $1 trillion, when we tally total federal, provincial, municipal, and crown corporation debt, as well as all unfunded government liabilities.

Because all forms of government debt are really just a form of deferred taxation, this means we have broken a bond with future

generations by obligating the unborn, who are not here to defend themselves, to pay for services consumed by the present generation. We are
consigning them to a form of fiscal slavery, or bonded labour. All free
and responsible societies of the past have attempted to improve things
for the next generation, not improve their own generation at the expense
of the next. This is an execrable, profoundly immoral act that is weakening the entire nation. It is felt in higher unemployment, a shrinking
asset base for all, a falling standard of living, and a kind of dispiriting
lassitude. Indeed, one province, Quebec, is already attempting vigorously to escape this worsening reality. More could well follow.

The blunt fact is that Canada's total debt has been borrowed to
facilitate the growth of innumerable government programs that the
people were obviously unwilling to fund, in the soul-numbing belief that
government ought to provide as many services as possible, in the belief
that what I have elsewhere described as the "top-down" state ought to
replace the "bottom-up" society at every opportunity.

A top-down state is based on the belief that all the needs of the
people must be administered for them by governments, and that this will
create a unified, harmonious society. The bottom-up model, on the other
hand, proceeds from the opposite belief: that government ought to set
the rules, and referee the game, but never play it; that people must be
respected as self-reliant moral agents capable of looking after themselves in the fullness of an orderly freedom.

The argument used by defenders of the top-down state is that social
spending helps the needy. But about 70 percent of Canada's so-called
social spending is in fact transferred to middle- and upper-income Canadians. Fully 33 percent of all government spending is transferred to the
top third of income earners! For culture and recreation services, the
figure is 47.4 percent, for health spending, 37.6 percent, and for education, 42.5 percent. This is shocking testimony, indeed, and serves to
remind us that the most common product of any regime that aims to
replace personal initiative is big government with massive debt.

I propose first, therefore, in the interests of harmony and unity, to
radically *de-politicize* and *re-federalize* Canada by vigorously promoting a return to our roots. Our wise founders, creating this nation at a
period of history that had just witnessed the Terror of the French Revolution (mounted in the name of egalitarian democracy) and then the

bloodbath of the American Civil War (fought to defend democratic states' rights), feared rampant democracy as well as the tyranny of big government. They envisioned Canada as a balanced set of sovereign provinces within a sovereign nation. Our British North America Act of 1867 reflected their vision in its strict division of federal and provincial powers, a division intended to check the growth of government by forbidding federal involvement in certain provincial affairs, such as health and education, and in turn inhibiting the excessive power of provincial governments by forbidding them to borrow beyond their own "sole credit." Each province was to live within its own means. But these wise restrictions have been aggressively circumvented in successive betrayals of our own constitutional limitations.

These betrayals of our founding vision were deliberately initiated, from the late 1960s onward, for the specific ideological purpose of strengthening federal and weakening provincial powers. Provinces in turn have rapaciously weakened traditional municipal powers. Ask any mayor.

This long process has everywhere disempowered, overregulated, and dispirited the people as a whole by robbing them of local initiative. Accordingly to Statistics Canada, we currently have not 1 government employee for every 15, or 18, or even every 10 citizens, as in many countries, but 1 for every 5.5 citizens! An honest calculation, removing dependent children under 18 from this number, would produce a figure closer to 1 government employee for every 3 productive citizens!

Canada is close to the disastrous situation of Sweden, where, for the first time in the history of the free world, we find a country the majority of whose citizens receive the bulk of their income from the state, in subsidies, or pay, or some combination of these two. It does not take a rocket scientist to figure out that when the majority of the citizens of any nation are beholden to government for their living, democracy, in any meaningful sense, is finished. The people will always vote for their paymaster.

So the radical *de-politicization* proposed here would restrict our federal government to a maximum of seven ministries to deal with truly national matters only, such as transportation and energy, justice and police, banking, communications, defence, foreign affairs, and internal affairs (not the close to forty ministries and sub-departments we had under Brian Mulroney). No further ministries could be created without leave of the people. Switzerland has run its federation this way for hundreds of years through a conscious effort to restrict big government, on the theory that no federation, regardless of size, needs more than this handful of federal ministries.

Re-federalization, in turn, requires a return to the strict division of powers of the BNA Act, precisely to curtail the growth of the sort of socialist-style government we now have. Unity and harmony will flow naturally from ten sovereign provinces in a sovereign nation, in which a people will feel united, not by universal medicare or welfare handouts, but by shared principles of liberty, self-governance, and spontaneous local community.

The ultimate purpose of both the above actions is to concretely free the people — indeed specifically require them by law — to look after their own lives and affairs within each province (our original BNA law), state (original U.S. law), or canton (current Swiss law), accordingly.

A corollary action required is the more philosophical idea of *subsidiarity*, which I would entrench in our highest constitutional documents. This term refers to the idea that concrete solutions to all human problems must be found at the *lowest* level at which the problem is generated, and no higher level of government may be invoked unless there is clear failure at the lower level. I would entrench this notion as a matter of national philosophy in our constitution, thus mandating a continuous devolution of power.

Accordingly, municipalities, provinces, and the federal government would be required to solve their own problems, each at their own level (as detailed in our constitution). Unfortunately, Canada's 1982 Charter of Rights and Freedoms reversed this commonsense prohibition on interference by placing a duty on the central government to equalize all citizens and regions through transfers and entitlements, thus offending our original subsidiarity principle. The predictable result was dependent regions, full of too many dependent souls. We now have one or two "giver" provinces, the rest "takers," and a population that has learned to make claims for so-called "positive" goods and services (meaning real things, such as cash subsidies or health care services) as rights to be delivered by governments (that is, by other citizens currently, or by future taxpayers). This has been a vast sea-change from all prior traditional concepts of free societies, in which citizens' rights were "negative," meaning that they were laws specifying what governments could *not* do to citizens.

Because of such deleterious effects, I would therefore *scrap our Charter of Rights and Freedoms*. This popular yet widely misunderstood document may yet ruin our nation, for reasons not yet clear to the people, who often defend their free democratic Parliament alongside the Charter that limits that freedom. From the moment the Charter became effective, every act of Parliament suddenly had to face possible judicial scrutiny to remain law. Suddenly, law-making in Canada meant a face-off between elected representatives and unelected judges. The most dangerous effect of the Charter, therefore, has been to neutralize the prestige of Parliament (ostensibly the voice of the people) by placing a Supreme Court of philosopher kings and queens in a supervisory position. I say this is dangerous because these judges cannot be dislodged by any power in the land, and whether from right, left, or the middle, they have the understandable habit of interpreting the abstract words of the Charter according to their personal political enthusiasms and beliefs. As a result, instead of merely judging conflicts or errors in law — what judges traditionally did — they now too often make law, by "reading into" abstract Charter words meanings that are not specified there.

Perhaps the worst effect of the Charter is that hundreds of interest groups, steered mostly by radicals who know the people would never vote for their programs, have quickly learned techniques for influencing the courts and the entire legal community via the faculties of law, through law journals, political-correctness programs for judges, and other organs designed to change law from the top and circumvent the democratic function of Parliament. These modern radicals hate democracy (the people and their values). But they love the Charter (which delivers their own radical programs). Scrapping the Charter would help neutralize all such interest groups. Not incidentally, I would scrap every penny of subsidy to all interest groups, including businesses.

The sad fact is that Canada's recent exercises in constitution-making — the Charter, the Meech Lake Accord, and especially the Charlottetown Accord — were not, properly speaking, constitutional. A true constitutional document must be about the rules and principles by which a people and their governments are permitted to make their deals. But it should never, never in itself, be a deal. However, all the aforementioned documents were just that. They resulted from deal-making and horse-trading between politicians and hundreds of disgruntled interest groups. A despicable spectacle.

So I would replace the Charter with a basic *constitutional amendment* to ensure the following: Canada's constitution shall refer to "citizens" only, and shall not distinguish among political groups of citizens in any way. In turn, the same laws shall apply to all citizens equally, and neither governments nor their agents shall be above any law (as many agents, agencies, tribunals, and commissions of government now are). Neither shall governments be permitted to act in ways forbidden to the citizens — for example, to discriminate, when citizens are forbidden to do so (as is not only permitted but encouraged under section 15). All forms of official discrimination by governments, at all levels, regardless of how "affirmative" in intent, shall be outlawed, on the grounds that we can never discourage immoral or unsavoury behaviour by practising it.

Basic rights to free speech, trial, property ownership, justice, trade, religion, and language use shall be defended vigorously, in keeping with the common-law traditions of our people. Our one-sided, inefficient program of official bilingualism would be scrapped and official language mandates devolved to the provinces (Quebec has already managed this). Further, there shall be no "constitutional ranking" among groups of citizens by gender, ability, colour, race, religion, or any other feature of humankind. Neither shall Canada's constitution mandate any social engineering via economic transfers (as it does now), or via claims or rights, among persons or regions. The idea of freedom of opportunity must be protected and promoted, not the debilitating notion of equal outcomes or social goods as national entitlements. The immediate effect of this change would be to transform regions and provinces from stagnating recipients of redistribution into competitive entities, each vying to please the citizen taxpayer.

Finally, I would propose that all *residual powers* (all things not specified in the constitution) revert to the provinces, and not, as currently, to the federal government. This is a most important way to institutionalize our devolution of power, because it means that any new task requiring government action not specifically mentioned in the constitution would have to be managed provincially, not federally.

The general idea of rights in our constitution must be defined explicitly as *negative*, not *positive* rights, on the grounds that the key function of a good constitution must be to protect the people from encroaching power. It must stipulate openly that such encroachment — which always erodes subsidiarity — is the greatest danger to their political and economic freedoms, especially to their ability to produce such goods and services for themselves through free markets and private initiative. In other words, this key constitutional amendment must stress *immunities*, not *amenities*!

The highest political documents of any people *must reflect their basic values*. In Canada, they do not. The Canadian people as a whole have never been socialist, collectivist, or for that matter redistributionist in their thinking or traditions. But their modern elites have. At heart, when pressed to articulate their philosophy of life, Canadians more often than not say that they believe in what I call "the Four Fs": Freedom, Family, Free Enterprise, and Faith.

By this I mean that, regardless of their political party, Canadians will normally defend the idea of individual freedom and the notion of persons behaving as moral agents in pursuit of the good life. This is what they teach their children. While they will defend any individual's right to live as he or she wishes, they will also fight hard for the traditional idea of the natural family as a married mother and father living together with their dependent children. They are deeply disturbed by the strenuous efforts of governments to dilute this definition, effectively ending traditional family protections in law and social policy.

They also very much resent the endless march of higher and higher taxation, and more and more regulation of enterprise, whether through income taxation, special corporate levies, wealth taxes, or the GST (which, they half joke, means "Go South Today"). For many businesses, governments are now dictating who must be hired (employment-equity quotas), how much to pay them (minimum-wage and pay-equity requirements), and how much may be charged a customer (price ceilings in many categories of business). Such multi-level controls eventually spell the end of free enterprise.

And finally, because about 90 percent of Canadians declare themselves to have a faith in God (and 90 percent of those say they are "Christian"), they are frightened that governments have so carelessly marched against their free expression of religious belief, both in the public square and in the public schools, despite the fact that the Preamble to our present Charter states that Canada "is founded upon principles that recognize the supremacy of God and the rule of law." (This is God's one and only cameo appearance in Canadian constitutional documents.)

In short, Canadians continue to believe there is a law higher than government, by which they try to live, however inadequately. This single belief is itself indelibly connected to their belief in civic freedom, for once firmly under God's law, you can never be wholly under Caesar's. Every nation in history that banned the fourth "F" soon became a tyranny. There are no exceptions.

For all these reasons, our constitutional amendment must include our commitment to these four pillars. We must defend them vigorously, repudiating and reversing in every way the explicit welfarism, economic dirigism, and rights-philosophy found in our current Charter. This will be a traditionalist initiative of the highest order, through which the people insist that their highest political document must reflect their society, not the state. The state must be the servant of society, not the reverse, and our constitutional amendment must specifically require this.

As for our institutions themselves, I believe the House of Commons should continue to be representative by population, and the voting method used to send representatives there must be altered to ensure majority rule. We should never have the situation, so common to our first-past-the-post system, wherein the simple arithmetic of voting may result in the whole people being governed by a minority. This possibility defeats democratic philosophy at its very heart, creating public disrespect for democracy.

As for the Senate, or second house, the basic purpose of which is to check the impulsivity of Parliament, I believe the provinces should be represented there equally, whatever the total complement may be, thus protecting small provinces from oppression. Traditionally, second houses are comprised of gifted citizens — architects, not bricklayers — appointed for their leadership qualities. They are expected to deliberate on national issues from above the fray and pressure of party politics. In theory, appointment preserves them from party influence-pedlars. This is a fine ideal, aiming at wisdom not popularity, and one worth preserving. But in a corrupt society, where this ideal is impossible, a system of indirect election (by legislatures) may have to be used to fill the Senate, which would at least have the merit of diluting corruption.

This dilemma — between wisdom and popularity — suggests why a virtuous democracy boils down to culture, to the quality and ideals of the people, why public good depends on private virtue. For no institutional methodology for choosing leaders — whether by lot (as in ancient Greece), by universal franchise (as in Canada, where even criminals get to vote), or by random selection of candidates — will guarantee wise leadership if the people are not wise.

Which brings me to the matter of *direct controls* over government. Democracy, as we know, may be direct: the people themselves vote on all law, as in some ancient Greek cities, in the early New England colonies, and in some Swiss cantons today. Or, it may be indirect, as is usual in large federations, where we delegate this law-making responsibility to chosen representatives.

Let it be said that there is no particular guarantee of wise choices from either method. Leaders may be wise or corrupt, and so may the people. If wise, representative democracy is certainly more efficient. The people may tend their cows and hat shops, while their delegates tend to government.

But if representatives promote a system of laws increasingly opposed to the core values of the people, as at present, there will always be a clamour for direct control. The people call for lower taxes. They are raised. The people call for capital punishment for heinous crimes. About 1,200 convicted murderers walk about on parole, and so-called young offenders burgle, rape, and murder with near impunity. The people call for more emphasis on family values. The whole concept is diluted beyond recognition. Fully 94 percent want standardized evaluation in schools. They cannot get it. And on it goes. So it is no surprise that we see a high level of distrust and disgust, and that the people want to make the laws themselves, or at least be able to revolt against their governors by firing and replacing them at will.

For this reason, and provided the methodology is sufficiently arduous to dissuade simple cranks from using it, I would institute *referendums* on basic national questions — especially those dealing with taxation, budgets, and government action and size — so that the people as a whole could "own" their democracy. The best rebuttal to critics of the referendum technique is that if the people find they have made a stupid choice at any one time, they may alter it. Although individuals, as Edmund Burke put it, may often be stupid, given enough time and opportunity to correct themselves, the people as a whole will be wise.

I would also institute *"citizen initiatives,"* which means an ability of the people to generate a law their representatives have wilfully delayed or refused to make. The Swiss do this regularly. They may also annul a law their delegates have made by such procedures if they think it bad. This has the happy effect of checking power at its source and making most laws conservative in nature.

Also necessary in a corrupt age such as ours, where men and women perform politics as often for career and personal glory as to honour the laws and their nation, I would institute a recall procedure enabling the people to fire delegates who have committed proven malfeasance, or who simply have not done what they said they would do. For a politician, this ensures a healthy conflict between party and people that will give almost certain priority to the people and the "bottom-up" ethos that keeps democracy vital.

The Economic Solutions

A great insult to believers in the social welfare state is the philosophy of free enterprise: of individuals and their families left free to work as hard as they wish, to make as much money as they wish, to buy and sell what they wish, and otherwise determine their own economic futures. The insult arises from the fact that, in such a system, the people, through a kind of "dollar democracy," in effect determine economic outcomes for the whole nation. For the collectivist, who thinks he always knows best how to spend the earnings of others, this is sheer irresponsibility.

But I believe that for an enterprising people, there is very little a free market cannot be persuaded to make in abundance, provided there are willing customers. And if there are not willing customers, then why would anyone, especially governments, with their renowned inefficiency, make it? And so, as part of a general philosophy of limited government in a free society, excepting only certain basic services such as defence, police, and perhaps some aspects of infrastructure for transportation and communication, the free market must be encouraged to operate widely and imaginatively, with government's main purpose to protect both the market framework and the people from force or fraud. The opposite philosophy has been a disaster.

In 1960, Canadians surrendered about 30 percent of GNP to governments at all levels. Today, they surrender around 50 percent. Tax freedom day is now mid-June (mid-July if deficit repayment is included). Since 1960, the Consumer Price Index has risen 400 percent while the Consumer Tax Index has risen 1,200 percent. But our roads, though more numerous, are no better. The public schools are worse. And Canadians, despite a universal prepaid "health care" system that eats up more than a third of provincial budgets, are no more healthy than they were. Perhaps less so. Certainly bigger, fatter, weaker is the trend for each successive generation of children. For all this, we have our $1-trillion debt to show — a debt that is already restructuring Canada, whether we wish it or not.

Clearly, as governments cannot restrain themselves, they must be restrained by the people. This means we need a "fiscal guillotine," by which I mean a method to restrain or fire governments that plunge the people into debt. My suggestion is that in addition to *balanced budget legislation*, any government that runs a debt two years in a row may be put to election at the will of the people.

Further, and perhaps most radical of all in the service of a traditional society, central government should have *no right to tax citizens directly*, or if so, only at a minimal level fixed by referendum. It should receive the bulk of its funds as a fixed percentage of the Gross Provincial Product of each province, to be spent only on matters proper to it under the constitution, the common percentage to be decided periodically by the provinces and fixed by law.

I would also *end the "progressive" income tax* system so dear to the socialist set. It is plainly discriminatory, and discourages wealth-creation. It would be replaced with a simple *flat tax*, applicable to all (according to a wide variety of tax specialists, the optimum level for such a tax is about 24 percent). This would offer the further benefit of eliminating all "loopholes" and a byzantine, undecipherable system of tax accounting and law. Further to this, all taxation would be indexed, to avoid the invisible tax of inflation and its corresponding "bracket creep." All *capital gains taxation* would be eliminated in order to stimulate the buying and selling of properties and businesses now forestalled by the disadvantageous economics of taxation. Business deals ought to be executed primarily for market reasons, not tax reasons.

Many serious economists around the world are now arguing that the income tax ought not only to be changed but replaced entirely, because it discourages work. They favour a *general consumer tax*. You pay when you spend. This would likely create larger capital pools, therefore cheaper lending, thus stimulating business formation and simultaneously raising employment and the standard of living. I would recommend this as a second-stage reform.

Perhaps the most electric economic (and social) policy change would be a pro-family tax policy of allowing all married couples (only) to *split income before taxation* (to file what used to be called a "joint tax return"). This would instantly do away with the nefarious penalization of traditional married couples when one parent (usually a mother) wishes to stay home and raise the children. A husband earning, say, $60,000 per annum would report only $30,000, and his wife the same. Besides a handsome reduction in their total bill — about $7,300 less tax paid — such a policy would economically validate a mother's role in society, thus healing an old wound.

Other important pro-family changes would be to return to a system of vastly *increased dependent child deductions*. Currently, there is almost none. Instead, the government sends parents a cheque, a form of non-taxable child welfare payment (from $1,000 up to $2,000 per year, depending on circumstances). This should be increased to about $4,000 per child and deducted by the taxpayer, thus eliminating a branch of welfare. I would also implement *maternity bonuses* as Quebec has done, to offset the disastrous declining birth rate in Canada, now at only 1.65 children per woman (when the replacement rate required to stabilize any population is 2.1).

Other pro-family policies, designed to strengthen traditional society by discouraging single-parenting and common-law unions, would be to allow *full mortgage interest deduction*, as well as *50 percent higher RRSP contributions* for any legally married couple (not available to common-law couples) with dependent children under eighteen living at home. An important further feature would be a tax deduction equivalent

117

to the child deduction ($4,000) for *"same-home" care of sick or elderly parents* or other older relatives, or disabled people. And finally, in order to drive government out of family life, I would forbid all welfare — and unemployment insurance — for children of the rich (unless wards of the state), and for all individuals under twenty-five from families earning more than the average family income. Furthermore, unemployment insurance should be just that: a pool of capital fully funded by the workers themselves to insure them when out of work, not an unfunded general welfare scheme, as at present. My law would specify: if it isn't funded, you don't get paid. In general, because there is always a moral with the money, so to speak, we must focus on policies that drive individuals away from government dependency — government is broke, anyway — and towards work and their families.

The Social Solutions

Canada must stop using its equality-based Charter-style arguments about discrimination to spread formerly targeted and exclusionary social benefits to all citizens. All social policy is inherently and intentionally exclusive, and therefore discriminatory; you must qualify for it. For example, you cannot get a veteran's pension if you have not fought in a war. Married benefits require being married. Welfare requires straitened circumstances. And so on. The modern trend has been to call this exclusionism "discriminatory," and then spread benefits to all classes of people. But if social policy is not discriminatory, it is simply another form of general welfare. The important thing, therefore, is to decide in what direction we wish a policy to discriminate, and then make sure it does so.

In addition to the economic policies above that have obvious social ramifications, I would add these more narrowly social policies.

First, *divorce*. The idea of "no-fault" divorce has led to the idea of "no-responsibility" marriage. As a society we must stop thinking of the happiness or complaints of adult individuals and focus instead on the happiness and welfare of the nation's children, and of the social fabric of the nation itself. The idea that one party to a solemn agreement can dissolve it at will, whether or not the other — who may have honoured the marriage vow in every detail — agrees, is dangerous to all society. Responsibility and stigma against divorce must be reintroduced and, where children are born to the marriage, a longer waiting period, of, say, five years, required.

The matters of *abortion* and *adoption* policy must be considered together. Fully 70 percent of Canadians oppose abortion on demand, yet we have no law against unlimited abortion. Canada's open season on killing the unborn must stop, and a law must be created restricting abortion to the traditional reasons of incest, rape, unsustainable life, or likely death of the mother, decided by community jury. It is indefensible that control over the life or death of a defenceless unborn child should be decided by a single person. At the same time, adoption should be encouraged (and would be by the increased child deduction suggested above).

Concomitant with this, we need strong social stigma against *errant fathers* and a determined effort to force them to honour their parental obligations. The low standard of living in single-parent homes is due mostly to the absence of fathers. But paternity cannot be taken seriously when from early youth boys are informed that the life or death of their unborn child is the mother's decision alone; they can have no role in the matter. As it stands, the mother may kill the father's child if she wishes, without consulting him, but if she decides to give birth, she can claim financial support from the father for eighteen years. Rather, both mother and father ought to be responsible for the welfare of their child from conception. Failing this, we can expect a lot more abortion (already 27 per 100 live births in Canada; only 3 per 100 in 1970), illegitimacy (about 24 percent of all births; only 4 percent in 1961), negligent fathers (who knows how many?), a larger, very angry underclass, and more youth crime — now the most rapidly accelerating class of crime in Canada.

On the matter of *community moral standards*, it is important to understand that our Charter has had the effect of disempowering and discouraging local communities. Whether on the matter of sex education, religious teaching, or pornography, local communities have learned that protest is of little use because they and their communities do not count. Unknown judges, two or three thousand miles away, will decide. To counter this dangerous amoralism, we must permit municipalities and provinces to pass local laws governing their local communities. Laws governing moral behaviour should be "bottom-up," not "top-down," as at present. Mothers ought to be able to march on the local variety store to protect their kids from pornography — and get results. Better a fully engaged community and the diversity of standards that will result than no standards at all.

As things stand, in order to counter the current morals vacuum, people either give up. Or they cocoon. Or they dissociate from society. Or, if they can afford it, they send their children to private schools. Living standards correlate highly with educational level. Which lands me on one of the most important policy changes needed: *choice in education.* I believe that the whole idea of government-run schools is contrary to the values and principles of a free, private, and family-based society. Canada has no crisis in education; it has a crisis in public education. And when all is said and done, that is because public schools (no matter that there are some very good ones, usually in good neighbourhoods) must ultimately serve the state and its ministries, not the consumer of education, which is the private family.

Public school systems are so horrendously bureaucratized they too often fail to produce an educated child. In constant dollars, public education costs have gone up 300 percent over the past thirty years, and salaries up 50 percent. But dropouts are variously between 20 and 30 percent, according to who you read. Educational results are almost (intentionally, I think) unmeasurable. Radical, mostly leftist unions and bureaucrats control almost all educational policy and curricula. And illiteracy and innumeracy rates are shameful — up to 38 percent of the population, by current Statistics Canada measures, cannot attain the "everyday" level. After a century of effort, it is by now clear that public schooling is the most visible failure of socialism in North America.

That's why I would immediately implement a voucher system, permitting parents one voucher per school-aged child for the pro-rata amount of the education budget, to spend at any school of their choice, public or private. Such a method would end by semi-privatizing the whole system. Education would then reflect society, the community, and the private family, more than the government and its collectivist ideology. This is not a perfect idea, because it simply returns tax dollars to parents and only partially eliminates government. But importantly, it eliminates governments' worst effects by introducing immediate competition to a moribund school system. Bad teachers hate the idea, but good ones welcome it. Families in poor areas in America, such as Harlem, where it is being tried, especially like it. Over forty U.S. state legislatures currently have "choice in education" legislation on the books, struggling for passage against massive opposition from collectivist ideologues, education bureaucracies, and unions. (Speaking of unions, I would also invoke immediate "right to work" laws permitting employees to work without any obligation or pressure to join a union, and remove Canada's infamous "Rand formula," by which employees must pay union dues even if they choose not to join a union.)

Finally, most Canada-watchers have already figured out that our flagship social program, universal medicare, cannot withstand current debt pressure and restructuring. We already have long waiting lists for specialists in various forms of surgery, hospitals are amalgamating and shutting down whole wings, and researchers watch funding shrivel.

But the enormous monies spent on health care have little to do with health. There are many nations, such as Italy, that spend half the per capita amount on health care that we do and have a population just as healthy by any standard. So where is the money going, and for what?

My view is that we don't ask citizens to insure their neighbour's car, or house, or boat. They would be outraged at the thought. So why should we ask citizens to insure their neighbour's body? Clearly, free market insurance should be brought back at once. Let us free physicians and patients from government control. Let the governments' only role be standards of care, and a pool of insurance for catastrophic coverage of those too poor or careless to insure themselves.

The Unity Solutions

Disunity in any nation starts in a felt dissociation from core values and the public perception that political institutions no longer reflect these — in fact, that such institutions are poised to attack core values.

A sore point for most Canadians on the matter of unity is current immigration policy. My view is that Canada has had a historical struggle with one large ethnic group — the French — that may yet divide us. The voluntary importation of other large ethnic groups may cause the same sort of grief, locally or nationally. I would therefore lower all immigration intake to half the present level and impose a quota-system based on the current ethnic make-up of Canada, so as not to further upset our ethnic balance. This would bring an immediate reduction of anxiety to the public.

But there are much larger matters of unity. My basic contention is that the wholesale imposition on Canadians of a burdensome welfare-state ideology over the past three decades (an idea now entrenched in our Charter), with its concomitant (and utterly predictable) massive debt, has caused the erosion of our wealth-creating potential, a politics of envy, a rights-based society, and increased national discord. In such circumstances many provinces will naturally begin to weigh the costs and benefits of unity at the first opportunity. Nationhood, under such a regime, gets diminished to the dismal level of cost-benefit accounting.

Which leads me to the question of a province wishing to separate from Canada. Let it be said as simply as possible: all federations ought to have some mechanism to allow the separation of an unhappy part of the whole, on well-defined and preferably difficult terms that are agreeable to the whole. Canada's somewhat imprecise method for separation currently requires amendment of the constitution, and approval by seven out of ten legislatures having between them 50 percent of the entire population. Any other method is contrary to Canada's constitution. In fact, it is likely treasonous. That's because Canada's provinces, as they now exist, have no legal status except as provinces of Canada, and there is simply no existing national or international right for any part of a federation to break up the whole at will by a simplistic 50-percent-plus-one-vote referendum. Nor ought there to be. Even if permitted, a matter so serious ought always to require a special majority of 66 percent, or two-thirds of the whole people, to whom the whole country belongs.

That Canadians have not realized this is a serious sign of our detachment from the meaning of Confederation. Which returns me to the body of my argument. Quebec's eagerness for separation has heightened in the measure that Canada's interventionist, centralizing welfare state has increased its threat to the Quebec way of life. To defend itself at every turn, Quebec has therefore negotiated separate accords permitting it to run its own medicare system, pension plan, immigration system — you name it. What Quebec has always wanted is absolutely minimal federal interference. For what? Ironically, to run its own welfare state inside Quebec! Fine. I say let Quebec do it — but with Quebec's money.

And that is my proposal for the whole nation.

That was the proposal of our founders, who limited each province to borrowing funds solely on its own credit, thus hoping to stave off big government.

In other words, the basic idea of sovereign (or "distinct") provinces, in a sovereign nation, was written into our original constitution by our founders.

So it strikes me as timely and necessary that, by adopting the proposals given here, we could very well solve both Quebec's problem and our national problem of unity at one stroke.

For such a happy, harmonious reconstitution of Canada, we do not need to be radical, or visionary, or utopian.

We only need the courage to be ourselves.

TWELVE

REBUILDING A JUST CANADA

• • • • • • • • • •
BASIL "BUZZ" HARGROVE

*O*ne *of Canada's most outspoken advocates of social unionism, Buzz*
Hargrove is national president of the Canadian Auto Workers Union
(CAW). Born in Bath, New Brunswick, Buzz joined Chrysler in 1964 and
later became an executive board member of CAW Local 444. He became
a member of the CAW servicing staff in 1975 and was appointed assis-
tant to the Canadian director in 1978. As a negotiator, he has bargained
on behalf of unions representing workers in a number of sectors, including
automotive, aerospace, rail and air transport, and fisheries.

Derailing our National Dream

Canada is rapidly becoming a country of disappointed expectations and
unfulfilled potential.

A frightening contrast is emerging between what our society is
capable of achieving, and the poverty and inequality that are increasingly typical of the Canadian reality.

On the one hand, our nation is blessed with a tremendous wealth of
natural and human riches. We have land, and we have resources. We also
have know-how: the technical skills and experience that should allow
us to convert our natural resources into a healthy, enviable standard of
living.

Canada is an acknowledged technological leader, especially in
industries such as transportation equipment, electronics, and telecommunications. These technological advances allow us to produce more
goods and services with less work. Therefore, thanks to ever-greater productivity, Canadians should be able to enjoy a higher material standard

of living, as well as more leisure time in which to enjoy this affluence. Why, then, does the opposite seem to be occurring? The standard of living of most Canadians is actually *declining* year after year, despite the promise of the new technologies. Statistics Canada data show that average family disposable income declined for four straight years through 1993, falling by 7 percent (after inflation) from 1989. Most observers think that this decline has continued through to 1995.

Worse yet, this decline in the *average* level of family income masks a sharp polarization of income distribution and a growing gap between the rich and the poor. The National Council of Welfare recently reported that poverty rates in Canada grew dramatically in 1993, despite the economic recovery that had already started by then. Almost 5 million Canadians lived in poverty in 1993, up by 12 percent from the previous year. With continued high unemployment, and cutbacks in public social security programs, this figure has probably worsened even further since then.

Even for those who have been lucky enough to keep their jobs, wages and salaries have often failed to keep up with inflation, let alone the increasing tax bite of government. And instead of having more time off to enjoy the fruits of our new productivity, many Canadians are working longer hours than ever: Statistics Canada data show that the incidence of both overtime and moonlighting have increased notably in the 1990s.

Perhaps 2 million Canadians (1.5 million officially unemployed, along with under-employed workers and those who have simply given up looking) cannot find enough work. Many of the rest of us are working longer and longer just to make ends meet. Where are the fruits of our new productivity?

In sum, an ever-growing number of Canadians do not have access to the economic and social opportunity that is required in order to build a better life for themselves and their families. Their economic well-being, their family life, and their health are being sacrificed — even as the productive capacity of our economy grows steadily year after year.

Private Poverty, Public Poverty

The poverty and stagnation that are increasingly typical of private households have also become dominant trends in our public sector.

126

Canada's esteemed network of public health care and social security has come under fierce downward pressure. Our strong public infrastructure (producing skilled workers, transportation, and communication services that greatly enhance the efficiency of private business) is stagnating due to lack of funds.

In 1994, government consumption and investment spending shrank to a smaller share of total GDP than in 1971. The dramatic cuts in program spending now being implemented at all levels of government will sharply undermine our public sector even further. Equity, security, and access to opportunity — those features of our society that placed Canada at the top of the United Nations' ranking of countries according to their level of social development — are now very much in danger.

Despite the fiscal crunch, however, there is one line item in government budgets across the country that swells larger year after year: massive interest payments to generally well-off financial investors and bond-holders. By 1996–97, the federal government (despite the finance minister's tough talk on deficits) will pay over $50 billion per year in interest payments to investors — much more than any other item in its budget.

Historically high real interest rates (which in turn have contributed mightily to chronically slow economic growth) have been the cause of this shift in budgetary emphasis away from useful programs and towards huge interest hand-outs. Taxes for most Canadians have gone up, yet the real services they receive in return have been eroded; the difference has been kept by the financiers, who have profited handsomely from Canada's debt crisis.

Canadians are told that we simply can no longer afford the public programs that we once took for granted, no matter how important these programs have been to our quality of life. This is painfully ironic, since most of these programs — medicare, universal pension, unemployment insurance, affordable post-secondary education — were put in place during the 1960s and 1970s, when Canada's economy was far less productive than it is today.

We could afford to introduce and indeed expand these programs in decades gone by. The average federal deficit during the years 1950–80, when our public sector reached its zenith, equalled only 0.3 percent of Canada's GDP. In short, we managed to virtually balance our books, despite introducing a wealth of public programs that have been essential to the development of the free and fair Canada that we know today.

If we could afford these programs twenty years ago, we can certainly afford them today. The problem is not a shortage of wealth in this country. The problem is the way in which our growing wealth is controlled and distributed.

As we continue to debate the minutiae of public policy in our legislatures and in the opinion pages of our newspapers, Canadians must not lose sight of this central, overarching contradiction: our economy is capable of producing more wealth with less effort than ever before, yet most Canadians have seen their standard of living (in both their private lives as well as in the public sphere) decline year after year.

Dividing Canada

One bitter result of the economic stagnation that has gripped our nation for fifteen years has been a general rise in social tension, hatred, and prejudice within our society.

Naturally it has been the problem of national unity that has captured the most headlines. Indeed, economic stagnation has exacerbated regional and linguistic tensions within Canada. Federal cost-sharing measures (such as support for provincial health, education, and welfare payments) have been part of the glue that cemented Canada as a nation during the post-war era. As support for these programs is eroded, the incentive within each region of Canada to identify with a national rather than a regional interest is correspondingly weakened.

I believe that revitalizing fiscal federalism in Canada will be an important part of maintaining the collective willpower to hold our incredible, diverse nation together. But this will be impossible if the federal government — the only body in our society with the reach and breadth of interest necessary to design and support unifying Canada-wide economic and social initiatives — remains starved of the fiscal power with which to implement them. Lower interest rates and a revitalization of economic growth (and hence tax revenues) are preconditions for a positive resolution of our national unity problem.

A country with little commitment to the social and economic well-being of so many of its citizens is hardly a country that citizens in Quebec — or in other regions, for that matter — will be too excited about preserving. We need to revitalize the co-operative, caring spirit that helped to pull this country together if we are to successfully hold it together.

But regional and linguistic conflicts are not the only unity problem we face in Canada. Deep divisions between neighbours and co-workers, not just between provinces, is another legacy of economic stagnation, chronic unemployment, and the omnipresent ideology of competition that has come to dominate our culture. As family incomes decline, and as economic opportunity for a large segment of our society seems to fade over the horizon, many Canadians have turned their anger and their frustration against each other, rather than against the economic system that has failed them.

There has been a general decline in tolerance, a wide-ranging rise in racism and sectarianism. Canadians who have suffered through our fifteen-year "permanent recession" seem almost happy, strangely, when they see *other* Canadians also suffer — as if that could somehow lessen their own pain. Low-wage or unemployed workers cheer when the federal government slashes 45,000 civil service jobs: "It's about time they also suffered," they reason, instead of turning their attention to finding a way out of the mess for all of us.

There is a nasty, mean-spirited mood in the land — a red-neck revolution in the making. Instead of blaming the financiers who have profited from high interest rates and zero inflation, average Canadians are turning against each other. White male workers — whose economic fortunes have declined dramatically as a result of chronic unemployment, de-industrialization, and the weakened state of unions — blame the symbols of affirmative action instead of the real economic powers-that-be.

Having largely given up on the hope that government can do anything to improve their own lives, many working people have turned their attention to hating anything to do with government — and against government's feeble efforts to ensure that what remains of the "affluent society" is at least shared a bit more fairly among us all.

This is the source of Canada's greatest national unity problem. We need not only to rework federalism to keep our *country* together, we also need to rework and revitalize our ideas about community, in order to keep our *society* together. We need to defeat the pessimistic, "me-first" attitude that has become so prevalent, lest Canada be divided into a million lone, privatized solitudes, not just two. We need to reinspire the notion that Canadians can act together to improve our common well-being.

Who Has the Power?

Ironically, we cannot blame government alone for the failure to translate our tremendous economic potential into social reality. It is a natural reaction to pin the responsibility for economic or social failures on the governments that are entrusted to guide our overall social and economical development. But the trend in policy-making over the past fifteen years has been so dominated by a bias towards *deregulation* and *privatization* that it has become highly questionable whether our governments any longer possess the tools they need to put Canada back on track.

The operating principle of this trend in government policy is that "the market knows best." Government should not involve itself in our economic and social lives. Individual economic agents (such as individual businesses or consumers) know best how to promote their own economic interests. A free, competitive marketplace will magically channel these self-interested desires, via the famous "invisible hand," into a decentralized outcome that rewards the fittest and most productive amongst us.

At best, it is argued, government should simply establish a fair and stable "playing field" (by ensuring price stability and investor confidence, for example). Then government should stand back and watch the marketplace perform its wonders.

Governments in Canada have implemented one item after another of this free-market agenda over the last several years: deregulation of our energy, transportation, banking, and communications industries; free trade with the United States and Mexico, and the deregulation of foreign investment; privatization of dozens of crown corporations (including Air Canada, Petro-Canada, and now Canadian National). Public services have been downsized, taxes have been cut for well-off households and many corporations, inflation has been wrestled to the ground.

In short, Canada should now be an optimal testing ground for the free-market experiment. Corporate Canada has been granted a great deal of what it has asked for (through powerful lobby groups such as the Business Council on National Issues). Government has implemented deregulation, privatization, free trade, near-zero inflation, and a leaner, meaner public sector. But where are the results?

Yes, Canadians should demand more of their government — demand that action be taken to ensure that the benefits of economic growth and productivity are more widely and fairly shared. But Canadians should also be turning their attention to the power behind the throne: to the corporations and businesses who promised that their activity would expand, their payrolls would grow, their investments would multiply.

In reality, Canadians have been suffering through a period of prolonged stagnation that rivals that of the 1930s. The recession that began in 1990 was the longest and grittiest in Canada since the Great Depression. It was a "man-made" recession, induced by the industrial restructuring accompanying free trade and by super-high interst rates that were supposed to bring about the zero-inflation nirvana.

Meanwhile, at the micro-economic level, most industries that were deregulated have since suffered from chronic excess capacity, huge corporate losses, lay-offs, and declining wages. Even in the high-wage, high-technology industries that were supposed to benefit from restructuring and free trade, investment and employment trends have often been negative. For example, Canada's important electrical and electronics industries have lost 30 percent of their jobs since 1989, while our trade deficit in this vital sector has soared to well over $10 billion per year.

We are told to be patient: it will take time for the benefits of deregulation and free trade and zero inflation to be realized. But the economic recovery since 1991 has been the weakest in post-war history. Only in a single year (1994) has our economic performance come even close to matching the *average* growth that we experienced in the first thirty years after World War Two. Our economy had barely climbed back to its pre-recessionary peak (in terms of GDP per capita) when it stalled again in 1995 and entered what may be another recession.

Corporate Canada has failed to live up to its side of the bargain. The free-market environment is here in all its glory, but the economic benefits that Canadians were promised have failed to materialize. It is increasingly difficult to blame government for this poor performance. The corporate agenda has been implemented, but the corporations themselves have not delivered.

The Marketplace Is Not Enough

The free-market model looks great on paper in first-year college economics textbooks: let the market do its job, and supply will always equal demand. The invisible hand will always work.

The problem with this recipe in practice is that it ignores so many of the non-market forces that are also key ingredients for economic success. Yes, in many cases, competitive firms operating in a market environment are indeed capable of the innovation and production necessary to supply Canadians with the goods and services that they need and desire. But that competitive process operates within a physical and social context, one that may not automatically be conducive to healthy and fair economic growth. Corporate Canada has ignored the importance of government's continuing role in setting the stage for economic progress.

For example, private profit-maximizing firms can be very efficient at cutting production costs. But regulation and guidance — at both the micro and the macro level — are needed to ensure that this ongoing drive for greater efficiency is ultimately beneficial to society.

Who will ensure that this cost-cutting does not risk the health and safety of the workers, who are required to work harder and faster? Who will ensure that Canada collectively has the skills and technological base needed to compete in the most valuable emerging industries? Who will ensure that Canadians have the purchasing power to buy the products that are produced with ever-greater efficiency?

Left to its own devices, the free market will in many cases run up against a constraint that is fundamentally rooted in the profit-maximizing, self-interested nature of competition. Competitive firms will act effectively in their own self-interest. But there is no structure to organize and manage the *collective* interest. And with no attention to the collective interest (of entire industries or communities), ultimately the individual self-interest of all market players can be undermined.

For example, there are some specialized industries in Canada that are held back by a lack of highly skilled personnel. But individual firms are unwilling to take on the high cost of training new workers and apprentices, because they rightly fear that their competitors may simply hire away these valuable, newly trained employees. As a result, the development of the whole industry is held back: the self-interest of individual firms inhibits the well-being of the industry as a whole.

In this case, you need a public agency to impose some form of co-operative solution to the training problem on the individual firms that are incapable of finding a collective way out of their dilemma. This co-operative solution could take a variety of forms: public support (financed through taxes) for public institutes of higher education, or a regulatory requirement that every firm must spend a certain proportion of its income on in-house training (thus eliminating the "free-rider" problem described above).

Similarly, every firm and household would like to reduce its own taxes and thus maximize its own after-tax income. But if the public sector is starved as a result, then the social and physical infrastructure begins to crumble, and the *private* costs of *all* firms may increase. Canada's socialized health care system is widely recognized as contributing to the competitive advantage of Canadian-based firms (by reducing the cost of employer-paid fringe benefits), but exactly the same effect is also generated by many of our other public programs.

Without these forms of public management, the all-knowing, highly efficient private market system easily becomes bogged down in its own self-interest. The key to revitalizing Canada's economy, and to ensuring that the fruits of economic growth can indeed be enjoyed by most Canadians, is to resuscitate the general notion that smart public interventions play a crucial and valuable role in fostering a balanced and socially beneficial pattern of industrial development.

Canada's entire history is itself testimony to this wisdom. Had it been left to the free market, Canada would never have formed as a country — let alone managed to develop the economic and social infrastructure that now underlies our vast current potential as a nation.

Self-interested private firms alone could not have built a Canada-wide railway; opened up frontier lands through the provision of transportation, communication, and social and administrative services; provided world-class health and education services across regions and social classes, thus generating a well-skilled, productive workforce.

Our most valuable industries, too, would not have developed here had we left everything in the hands of free markets. Our automobile, transportation, electronics, and communication industries all gained their first footholds in Canada thanks to smart and timely public interventions — through the Auto Pact, the formation of Air Canada, or the public regulation of telephone services.

In the current rush to the free-market promised land, our highly positive experiences with the leading role of public intervention, economic co-operation (rather than competition), and conscious economic planning have all been forgotten. The chronic stagnation and growing inequality that have characterized Canada's economy over the last fifteen years are hard proof that the free market solution is not working.

In contrast, the rapid economic and social development of many East Asian nations — which have relied heavily on public investments, the regulation of capital markets, managed trade, and interventionist industrial policy — provides further proof of the potential benefit of smart public planning.

Let me therefore conclude by proposing a few ways in which a better balance between co-operation and competition, between private and public, could help Canadians to better realize the potential offered by our abundance of natural and social wealth.

Put Production Before Finance

Governments need to re-regulate financial markets to restore the incentive for investment in real productive enterprises, rather than unproductive or speculative financial assets. At present, extremely high interest rates provide investors with a greater reward for purchasing risk-free government bonds than for investing in the production of real goods and services.

In 1994, for example, the average return on equity for non-financial business in Canada (according to Statistics Canada) was 7.4 percent; these investments are inherently risky, and 1994 was a good year. In contrast, the average long-run rate of interest on virtually risk-free bonds was closer to 9 percent. As a result, new investment in the *real* economy has fallen dramatically as a share of GDP, compared with the lower-interest 1960s and 1970s.

In short, investors have become lazy and "dependent" on easy government money; they have lost the incentive to undertake the real work of capital: developing products, hiring labour and equipment, and marketing. We need lower interest rates to put capital back to work in a real job.

Our current high interest rates are not a "natural" result of financial markets, nor do they reflect any real risk of inflation or government default. Rather, they reflect a deliberate strategy by central banks and private financial interests to slow economic growth and enhance the value of financial assets at all costs. They have hamstrung our economy, and are bankrupting our governments. Interest rates must come down — even if this involves new regulations governing the operation of our financial system.

Nurturing "Community Entrepreneurship"

Growth and employment in our current system are strictly limited by the requirement of high profitability on private investments. Production opportunities must offer more than a *positive* return to investors: they must offer a high enough return relative to other appealing options (such as risk-free government bonds, or super-profitable investments in low-wage foreign countries) to justify new investment in Canada.

Thus our economy is held hostage to the demands of footloose investors (be they purely financial investors, or real businesses). We are pressured to cut wages, cut taxes, raise interest rates — or capital will leave. In the long run, the only way to reduce the dependence of our entire community on a small minority of investors is to start doing the job of investment ourselves.

We need to develop a tradition of "community entrepreneurship." By this I do not refer solely to the small-business initiatives of many community development programs. Rather, I am thinking in the broader sense that our communities need to take on collective responsibilities for doing many of the things that we presently rely on a few private investors for: developing technology and product ideas, raising and investing capital, hiring workers, and organizing production.

Our technical schools and universities generate valuable techno-logical innovations. Our workforce is skilled and motivated, but vastly under-utilized. Our economy could generate billions of dollars in new investment finance if employment (and thus household incomes) could be increased, and if proper regulations could be implemented to keep new funds circulating in the domestic economy rather than being side-tracked into the pockets of financiers.

Public and co-operative agencies could play a leading role in combining these valuable inputs and revitalizing our industrial base. This strategy would build on Canada's long and successful tradition with co-operative and public economic development initiatives — ranging from the public's role in building the first cross-country railway, to prairie agricultural and marketing co-ops, to strategic public investments in high-risk, high-value industries such as aerospace.

There are many specific policies that could be introduced to further this process of community entrepreneurship. These could include social investment funds to stimulate strategic high-value manufacturing industries; other public or community financial institutions generating pools of capital that are "loyal" to Canada (such as credit unions or public auto insurance funds); and industrial partnerships that link private and public investments, community know-how, and the skills of workers in new and productive enterprises.

The starting point shared by all of these initiatives is that Canada's economy is vastly *underperforming* — our rich base of physical and social resources is not being used at anywhere near its full potential, undermined by the demands of private firms for super-profits. In this case, Canadians can collectively step into the void and do the job ourselves: take our economic destiny into our own hands and accept the responsibility to combine our resources in a manner that is both economically efficient and socially beneficial.

Sharing the Time

One response to the ongoing growth in the productivity of our economy must be an ongoing reduction in working hours. Without shorter working time, consumer and export demand (especially in light of high interest rates and stagnant wages) cannot keep up with the greater quantities of goods and services that our economy can produce, and thus higher productivity simply produces higher unemployment.

Average working time can be reduced in many different ways. A shorter work week, longer vacations, early retirement, and reductions in overtime all serve to reduce average work time and hence create jobs.

But none of these measures will be introduced via the free market alone. In fact, left to themselves, profit-seeking firms have an incentive to *increase* working hours: by stretching out the work week, firms reduce the hourly costs of employment benefits paid to full-time workers. Sadly, many workers all too willingly accept the overtime, trying to make up for the stagnation of their basic hourly wages with longer hours on the job.

Governments must step in with incentives and regulations to reduce average hours, encourage vacations and early retirement, and curb overtime. Businesses will complain loudly about this interference in the "free market" — just as they did when the first rules to limit working time were introduced to curb the eighty-hour work weeks of the Industrial Revolution. But they will soon find ways to operate profitably within the new set of legal constraints; more importantly, the resulting new jobs will allow a greater number of Canadians to share the fruits of our ever-greater productivity.

Conclusion: Rebuilding Democracy

I have outlined a set of policies that I believe could rejuvenate the principle that smart and timely public interventions can make a crucial and positive difference to our collective economic and social prospects. But in reality, the most important task facing Canadians is not simply to choose a prime minister who advocates the best set of policies.

The fact is that most governments (of all political stripes) now seem to do the same thing — slash and burn the public sector — regardless of what they promise, and regardless of what the voters want. The huge contrast between the Red Book election program of the federal Liberal Party and the policies that the Liberal government introduced upon taking power is the most glaring example of this phenomenon, but it is hardly unique.

We seem to have a new democracy in Canada. Powerful financial interests, not Canadian voters, decide what governments do. The new democracy is limited to a process of sham consultation, in which Canadians are given the opportunity to air their views on where governments should cut, not on *whether* or not there are other ways of solving our fiscal crisis.

Our first task, therefore, is to rebuild the collective will to implement the policies that we choose, despite the opposition we may face from the most powerful elements of our society and economy. That is the role of the prime minister: to convince Canadians that poverty and selfishness are not inevitable. To show that we can do things *together* (not just as privatized economic maximizers) to improve our collective well-being. To demonstrate that we can influence our collective destiny despite the omnipresence of free markets and globalization.

Many Canadians have become cynical and hateful about governments. Simultaneously, they have become cynical about the very idea of doing things together. What we really need is a prime minister who will turn that around, who can show that Canadians can still work together, with the help of public and co-operative institutions, to rebuild Canada as a genuine and caring place of community.

THIRTEEN

JEAN CHRÉTIEN'S OPPORTUNITY AND RESPONSIBILITY

• • • • • • • • • •
JOHN CRISPO

John Crispo is a professor of Political Economy in the Faculty of Man-agement at the University of Toronto. He is the founder of the Uni-versity of Toronto's Centre for Industrial Relations and a member of the C. D. Howe Policy Analysis Committee. John Crispo has written a number of books, including Free Trade: The Real Story, Can Canada Compete? *and* Making Canada Work: Competing in the Global Economy. *He is a frequent media commentator on a wide range of social, economic, and political issues.*

WHAT A TIME TO BE THE PRIME MINISTER OF CANADA! While Jean Chrétien faces major constitutional, social, and economic challenges, he has ample political power to deal with them and thereby leave a very constructive mark on our country's history. Not only does he have a commanding majority in the House of Commons, but he is confronted by a divided opposition — the Bloc Québécois and the Reform Party, neither of which offers an effective opposition, let alone an alternative government.

Politics and the Art of the Possible

The question is whether Chrétien can provide us with better government than his two predecessors, Pierre Trudeau and Brian Mulroney, both of whom failed us miserably on the fiscal front, if not on other fronts, despite their massive majorities. (Note that I am not considering either John Turner or Kim Campbell, because neither was in power long enough to do us much good or harm.)

When I was an undergraduate, I was taught that in a democracy responsible government — perhaps in large part — depends upon having a meaningful opposition that offers a credible alternative. I hope and trust that Jean Chrétien will prove that this thesis is not universally applicable and will govern well in the absence of a real threat to his power, at least in the short run.

Chrétien is confronted by an equally great opportunity and responsibility. Given his strong majority and the disarray of the opposition, he has no excuse for not dealing with the major challenges — crises might be a better word — that we face in this country.

Before turning to these challenges, I want to make it clear that, in my view, Canada still has so much going for it that there is no reason, other than political, for us not doing well. Indeed, if we deal successfully with the challenges highlighted in this paper, Canada can remain number one in reputation as well as in fact. We will have only ourselves and those we elect to power to blame if we fail to take full advantage of this bountiful country of ours.

If Canada is to realize this potential, and if the nation is to achieve the related and more specific objectives reviewed in this paper, our political institutions must work more effectively. A few steps have been made in this direction by enhancing the role of the House of Commons Finance Committee in holding extensive open hearings as part of the budgetary process. Similar developments are required in every other area of public policy formulation. More transparency is required in all of our political decision-making mechanisms so that our elected representatives will be forced to focus less on crass political gamesmanship and more on the real economic and social issues that confront our country.

Quebec and the Future of Canada

The first challenge I would address as prime minister is the ongoing constitutional crisis revolving around Quebec's destiny in or out of the Canadian Confederation. On this front, Chrétien continues to play his cards well. He appears to recognize that this is a matter for Quebeckers to decide and that they would resent any heavy-handed federal intervention in what they consider to be their own debate.

It must be difficult and frustrating for a dedicated federalist like the Prime Minister to remain largely on the sidelines of this debate.

However, restraint is the wisest course of action. Like it or not, the rest of us in Canada must rely on the common sense of the Quebeckers to make the "right" decision on their own, only becoming involved when the federalists inside Quebec deem it appropriate for us to do so.

The problem is that even a vote by Quebeckers for Confederation will not end the matter. Maybe nothing will, not even a firm declaration by the rest of Canada that it recognizes that Quebec is different, special, and unique and that it treasures this fact of life. And such a declaration is not in the works, in spite of all the history and tradition that bears it out.

I'm not even sure that a hypothetical English-Canadian prime minister, one who was drawn from outside Quebec, could sell this reality to the rest of Canada. Assuming he or she could, the *quid pro quo* would have to be firm commitment on the part of the province of Quebec to the paramount importance of the federal government in such national spheres as defence, foreign affairs, monetary policy, and trade.

If Quebec votes for outright separation, or some hypothetical form of sovereignty-association, the Prime Minister will find himself in tremendous difficulty. It will be hard enough to hold the rest of the country together — British Columbia, or British Columbia and Alberta together, could be the next to pull out of a disintegrating Canada — let alone find some new accommodation with a Quebec that had voted for a radical change in Confederation as we know it now. Any red-neck, anti-Quebec sentiment that lies dormant in Canada would doubtless surface in a more virulent form than we have ever known it in the past.

How a French-Canadian prime minister would be perceived in such a confrontational situation is open for speculation. My feeling is that no prime minister — French-, English- or New-Canadian — could negotiate his or her way out of such a frightening impasse.

In this bleak scenario, nothing like the Canada we know would survive in anything like its present form. That is why we must hope and pray that the Prime Minister plays his federal hand astutely, and that Quebeckers decide that the evolving Confederation we have always experienced — not the *status quo*, which has never prevailed for long — represents a much better choice than the grave uncertainties associated with separation, sovereignty-association, or whatever else the Parti and Bloc Québécois choose to call their dream.

A Note on Our Growing Social Dream

The social crisis confronting this country takes many forms, only one of which I will briefly address here. I refer to the existence of a "less" generation — the so-called Generation X of twenty-year-olds and some part of the "baby boomer" generation. This group knows it cannot live as well as the previous "more" generation unless we turn this country around in relatively short order. If we do not, we could find ourselves moving into a virtual war between the generations, particularly when the post-war "baby-boomers" begin to retire. It is conceivable that they could end up living better in retirement than their children at work.

In the absence of a major economic resurgence in this country, it will not be long until the elderly — or "wrinklies" as the Australians like to call them — will be stretching our medicare and pension capacities to their breaking points. Regardless of how these various scenarios play themselves out, the resulting inter-generational strains and stresses could wreak havoc with the very social structure of our society. At both ends of the age spectrum, we could end up with some very embittered and disillusioned groups.

The most meaningful way to avoid this potentially explosive development is to get this country back on a sustained path of economic growth. This, in turn, demands that we continue to become more competitive both in the private and the public sectors of the economy.

Competitiveness as the Key

Increased competitiveness is the key to so many priorities in Canada that it should be the focal point of our public policy thinking. Only by becoming more competitive can we hope to generate, for example, more high-paying and secure jobs, a more rapid rate of growth, and a higher standard of living. Enhanced competitiveness is also vital if we are to generate the wherewithal to solve the following problems: Canada's massive government; federal and provincial deficits and debts; our deteriorating infrastructure; our environmental degradation; and, as already emphasized, our vulnerable medicare and social security systems.

In the broadest sense, competition today takes place as much between countries as it does between enterprises within different countries. To put it another way, no matter how well private enterprise does on its own in Canada, business could do better if it would operate within a sane, sensible, and sound public policy framework that allows it to plan ahead with certainty and confidence.

To begin with, this requires that Canada rid itself of as much instability and uncertainty as possible, because capital and investment shy away from societies that exhibit such characteristics. Much of this instability and uncertainty would fade away if we could get our constitutional and social houses in order. In this regard, of course, we are dealing with a vicious circle, since our difficulties in both of these areas stem, in considerable measure, from the under-performance of our economy. Fortunately, however, once one breaks into this vicious circle and begins to reverse it, improvements in each of the foregoing areas can reinforce progress in all the other areas.

The competitiveness challenge confronting the Canadian private sector can be put fairly succinctly. Basically, it is now required to serve a much more demanding customer, one who is insisting on better pricing, quality, and service. To begin to meet these demands, firms must treat their customers as kings before, during, and after any major sales. In order to do this, they must also treat their employees as kings, because they are the key to meeting the price, quality, and service demands of their customers.

Much less understood is the public sector's competitive challenge, which goes far beyond the need to provide the services it is responsible for delivering more efficiently, innovatively, and productively. If governments cannot meet this challenge through their existing departments and staff, they must be prepared to contract them out to private enterprises and their workers who can do so, if only because they have a bottom-line market test to meet.

Far more important, however, is for the provincial and local governments in Canada to get their public policies right so that the private sector can do its job better. To this end, every government policy should be reviewed to assess whether it is helping or hindering private enterprise to do the job that only it can do — that is, to create the economic basis for the well-being of the nation.

Coping with Our Fiscal Fiasco

At the federal level, the biggest problem is Canada's continuing large deficits and our growing and already massive federal debt, much of

which is now held abroad. It is essential that the Prime Minister confront these problems at a much faster pace than is called for in his
party's famous Red Book.

To this end, drastically reducing government expenditure should get
primary emphasis, as opposed to increasing government revenues. On
the revenue side, the answer is a radical reform of the taxation system,
the result of which would be neutral in terms of the funds it raises.

As for expenditures, nothing of great significance can be accomplished until we fundamentally change Canada's approach to virtually
all forms of social security — including compensation. Three basic
principles should underscore this change, the first being that no Canadians should be subjected to undue human degradation, poverty, or suffering through no fault of their own. This is an elementary principle in
any civilized society with the kind of wealth Canada enjoys.

The second basic principle is that all able-bodied Canadians in
receipt of any form of social security — except those in retirement —
should be expected to be doing something in return, either to improve
their own income-earning prospects or to help out their communities.
In the first category I would include taking advantage of retraining and
upgrading programs, as well as relocation assistance where there is no
hope of employment in one's current area of residence. The second category includes everything from voluntary community service to so-
called work-fare, some forms of which are essential for most
individuals' sense of self-esteem, self-respect, and self-worth as well as
the development and/or preservation of good work habits.

To facilitate participation in either of these alternatives, I would
offer day-care to single parents wherever it is available. As expensive
as this may be in the short run, it is bound to be a good investment in
the long run, especially if it helps families break out of the poverty traps
in which many find themselves.

The third basic principle involves a "claw-" or "tax-back" on all
forms of social security. No matter what one's source of social assistance, part or all of it should be taxed back as one's sources of other
income rise above a designated level. Mind you, this should not work
on a dollar-for-dollar basis if we want to leave any incentive for those
at the bottom of the income hierarchy to return to a self-sustaining
status without suffering what can amount to a financial penalty when

everything is taken into consideration.

The federal government could introduce these principles on its own, in areas where it is in full control of an existing social program (e.g., old age assistance and unemployment insurance). In others, it would require provincial co-operation. If it cannot secure such co-operation voluntarily, the federal government should not hesitate to make its new block-funding grant conditional upon the willingness of each of the provinces to adopt a similar set of principles, albeit with sufficient room for some experimentation.

The Case for a Flat Tax

As for taxes, I am prepared to contemplate a flat or single tax, despite the fact that I have always believed in a progressive income tax because of the ability-to-pay rationale. What has driven me to rethink my position is the abject failure of our present tax system, which fails every reasonable test in that it is no longer efficient, equitable, or simple. Provided we have a generous enough exemption on a flat or single tax, it will retain some progressivity while being much more efficient and simple to administer. If such a tax were applied to all forms of income and were revenue-neutral, it would come in at around 25 percent. It would have to rise by several percentage points if it were also used to replace the GST. However, that might still be worthwhile if it led to a significant cutback in the burgeoning underground economy.

If you combine what I have said about both Canada's social security system and its taxation system, you can see that it is not a big leap to the concept of a guaranteed minimum income based on a negative income tax, which would take the place of our existing plethora of income support systems. I would actually favour two guaranteed minimum incomes — one fairly generous for those individuals permanently out of employment through no fault of their own (i.e., those incapacitated or retired), and another, lower-level guarantee that would apply to those workers temporarily out of income because of injury or unemployment, leaving them with a strong incentive to return to work as soon as possible.

The Need for Competitiveness Assessments

Although I have concentrated on the delinquent fiscal policies of our recent governments, I would argue that everything they do should be subjected to competitiveness assessments. To illustrate my point, let me briefly touch on the issue of employment equity. Discrimination in employment is wrong, both economically and morally. In terms of redressing such discrimination, however, the pendulum has now swung too far the other way, so that we are now, in effect, imposing quotas and reverse discrimination. Instead, we should be concentrating on equal access and opportunity, whether in education, employment, or any opportunity relating to both one's potential contribution to society and one's consequent earning power.

To cite another illustration, consider the current environmental assessments. They are fine in principle but are often misguided in effect because they are so one-dimensional. Whenever we require an environmental assessment, it should be combined with a competitiveness assessment so that we weigh in the balance the inevitable tradeoffs between these two equally compelling criteria for our future well-being.

There is nothing our various levels of government are now doing that could not be improved by subjecting them to competitiveness assessments. Everything governments now provide — from education to medicare to investment and research and development incentives — should be reviewed to determine not only whether the purpose they serve is still of high priority but, equally important, how much more efficiently, innovatively, and productively they could be delivered.

Our Incompatible Complexes

Aside from the specific proposals I have offered the Prime Minister, I would urge him to help dispel two incompatible complexes with which Canadians can no longer live if they want to do well by their country and themselves. The first is the unwarranted inferiority complex so many Canadians suffer from in terms of their own abilities to compete, as well as the sense of inferiority felt by our enterprises and the country as a whole. This inferiority complex persists despite our fantastic export performance under the FTA and now NAFTA.

The other complex from which Canadians suffer is an insupportable entitlement mentality. While most Canadians now seem prepared to recognize that we have to reduce our deficits and debts, they do not want it done at their particular expense. It is, therefore, quite all right to cut off everyone else's entitlements as long as their own are not touched.

Obviously, we all have to give up something on the entitlement front if we are to put our fiscal house in order.

Securing Canada's Future

Let me conclude by reiterating that, in my judgement, there is no country on the face of the earth that enjoys more potential than Canada. Although we have been wasting much of that potential now for over a quarter of a century, this does not mean that we cannot reverse the situation in fairly short order. With the right kind of national leadership, we could be well on the way to doing just that before we enter the next century. Jean Chrétien has demonstrated that kind of leadership on the Quebec and trade fronts, but he has yet to do so on the critically important fiscal front.

If Jean Chrétien has the courage, insight, and willingness, he could put most of the federal public policy framework in order during his first term in office. Should he do so, he will deserve a second term. Then watch the private sector prove just how much it is capable of generating for Canadians, given the right public policy atmosphere and environment.

FOURTEEN

"IF I WERE PRIME MINISTER…": A "RECIPE" FOR RAISING LIVING STANDARDS AND UNITING THE COUNTRY

• • • • • • • • • •
MICHELLE FALARDEAU-RAMSAY, Q.C.

*M*ichelle Falardeau-Ramsay is the deputy chief commissioner of the Canadian Human Rights Commission. A native of Montreal, she holds a law degree from the University of Montreal and is a former senior partner with the firm of Levac and Falardeau. She is a former chairman of the Immigration Appeal Board and served as a human rights consultant to the United Nations operation in Somalia. She was also a member of the Canadian delegation participating in the bilateral observer mission for the South African elections. She is presently co-president of the International Day Committee for the Eradication of Poverty and chairperson of the board of directors of the Canadian Human Rights Foundation.

"It has been said that Canada is the most difficult country in the world to govern. I am perhaps more aware of that than I used to be."
— Prime Minister Lester B. Pearson, 1965

BEING ASKED WHAT I WOULD DO IF I WERE PRIME MINISTER is a little bit like being asked what I would do if I won a million dollars in the lottery, or what I would do if I met an alien from another planet. It is not likely to happen, so it is tempting to lapse into Utopian rhetoric about how to go about creating the perfect society.

Like Lester Pearson, having to grapple with this question has made me all the more aware of how difficult the task really is. As long as Canada is a democracy, and a federalist democracy at that, even the most well-intentioned prime minister cannot govern by whim. She or he is constrained by a wide range of factors: economic realities, which are impacted by factors far beyond our borders; the constitutional division of power between the federal government and the provinces; and public opinion.

This does not mean that one cannot attempt to skew these factors in one's favour. But to announce that I would attempt to return to the heady days of the 1960s, as much as I might like to in the best of all possible worlds, would be idealistic at best and counter-productive at worst. Similarly, calling for policies that are unrealistically centralist — such as transferring all responsibility for education from the provinces to the federal government — would not be feasible and would serve only to alienate the provincial interests, whose co-operation is essential to the establishment of a national vision.

Perhaps the best approach to this problem would be to take a tip from Mme. Jehane Benoit, the godmother of Canadian cuisine, whose comment on cooking is equally applicable to the business of policy-making. "I feel a recipe is only a theme," Mme. Benoit once wrote, "which an intelligent cook can play each time with a variation."[1] A would-be prime minister can put forward a recipe — an overriding theme that can be played with variations — and as long as those variations are in harmony with the central theme, the recipe will produce the desired result.

Let me also preface my remarks by saying that I do not purport to be an expert in either social or economic policy. I am not an economist, not a pundit, and not a policy analyst *per se*. My suggestions are the product of my experience: as a human being who has spent enough time on this planet to get a sense of what is going on around me; as a Canadian, with a passionate attachment to this country and all it stands for; as a francophone Quebecker, who has experienced the duality of Canada firsthand; as a woman, with the life experience all that entails; and as a lawyer who has devoted her career to labour relations, immigration, and human rights.

Finally, I believe that the two components of the question before me — "improving living standards" and "uniting the country" — are inextricably linked. It is easy in this country to over-emphasize the alleged barriers to unity: the historic tensions between French-speaking and English-speaking Canadians; the much lamented "lack of Canadian identity"; the tantalizing lure of American ways and American culture; and, more recently, the impact of multiculturalism. But in my view, none of these factors is as significant as the most pernicious division in our society: the gap between the "haves" and the "have-nots," between those who reap the benefits of the much-vaunted Canadian standard of living and those who are denied those benefits. We cannot forget that social and economic inequality were initially at the root of Québécois nationalism; that hostility towards immigrants and minorities is at its peak at times of economic uncertainty; and that if the American vision appeals to some Canadians, it is because of the illusion of prosperity that vision provides. This is exacerbated by a prolonged period of high unemployment, a growth in low-paid service-sector and part-time work at the expense of more highly paid permanent jobs, wage freezes for many employees, and fears that the social safety net is coming apart at the seams.

The relationship between standard of living and national unity was reinforced in a recent Decima Research report commissioned by the Canadian Council of Christians and Jews. One of the report's key findings was that 87 percent of Canadians feel that they are emotionally attached to Canada; however, 22 percent of those qualified that statement by professing to be "attached to Canada but only as long as it provides a good standard of living."[2]

In Quebec, the answers to this question were even more revealing. While roughly 25 percent of Quebeckers took the sovereigntist position ("would prefer to see Canada split up into smaller countries"), 67 percent professed an attachment to Canada. Of those, the Quebec respondents were evenly divided (33 percent vs. 34 percent) between those with an unconditional attachment and those for whom the attachment was dependent on a good standard of living.[3]

Thus, improving living standards and uniting the country are virtually one and the same: policies that lead to the former will ultimately result in the latter. And the fostering of unity, in turn, will also have a positive impact on living standards: a population that comes together as a community is more likely to come together to assist those in need. It is when individuals fail to see themselves as part of a community that they abdicate responsibility for the welfare of their fellow citizens. This leads to a culture of polarization and "me-first-ism," a culture that promotes selfishness over solidarity, individual gain over social progress, and social Darwinism over the fundamental principles of fairness and equity.

If I were prime minister, I would make every effort to strike a better balance: between rights and responsibilities; between fiscal restraint and social responsibility; between providing leadership and responding to public concerns; and finally, between respect for diversity and promotion of Canada as a community. This balance must be rooted in the shared values that bind Canadians together as a people: respect for human dignity, equal opportunity, and the belief that the state has some role to play in the well-being of its citizens. Made-in-Canada problems need made-in-Canada solutions, not "quick-fix" schemes imported from south of the border. Nor do we need ideologically driven solutions, from either the right or the left, which do little more than pit one group of citizens against another.

I do not intend to talk here about how to apply these principles to such diverse policy areas as the deficit, national defence, or the environment, none of which is within my area of expertise. But in an effort to move from the general to the more specific, the following would be my main priorities if I were prime minister:

Ensuring Equal Opportunity

If economic and social inequality are a primary source of disunity, ensuring equal opportunity, particularly in the area of employment, must be a primary goal. Needless to say, Canada has made some progress in this regard over the past two decades: our provincial and federal human rights laws — reinforced by the equality provisions of the Canadian Charter of Rights and Freedoms — are among the strongest in the world, and our efforts to promote employment equity, at least at the federal level, are ahead of most western industrialized countries. Women and visible minorities in particular have made significant progress in improving their representation in the workforce; in the case of women, this progress has been particularly evident in such professions as law and medicine and in the ranks of both private- and public-sector management. Unfortunately, the same cannot be said for aboriginal people and people with disabilities, who still have lower-than-average incomes and higher-than-average levels of unemployment.

A major challenge will be to continue to strengthen policies designed to foster equal employment opportunities, while at the same time responding effectively to allegations that such programs constitute a form of "reverse discrimination." This so-called backlash is at least partly the result of the overall economic situation, which sees more and more people competing for fewer and fewer jobs. Needless to say, government policies that result in job growth, essential for raising the standard of living, will also enhance equity efforts. So will government incentives for the development of small businesses and community economic development projects, especially since women, immigrants, and aboriginal people are increasingly involved in this sector of the economy.

But another component of the backlash is the failure by both governments and advocacy groups to ensure that employment equity programs are well understood by employers, employees, and the general public. If I were prime minister, I would direct the appropriate department, in consultation with business, labour, and advocacy groups, to find creative means of getting the message — and the facts — about employment equity out to employers, employees, and the general public.

Another aspect of ensuring equal opportunity is the provision of effective English- or French-language training for immigrants who are not proficient in an official language when they arrive in Canada. While I recognize that there are a variety of English- and French-as-a-Second-Language programs aimed at immigrants, there are often problems with accessing them, particularly for immigrant women. If I were prime minister, I would ensure that official language training was available to every new immigrant who requires it. This training could be administered by the federal government through Canada Immigration Centres; alternatively, it could involve setting standards for federal grants to provincially administered ESL and FSL programs.

Promoting "Diversity Bound by Commonality"

Closely related to the issue of equal opportunity is the question of how to foster diversity while, at the same time, promoting a common Canadian way of life. The same Decima survey that measured Canadians' attachment to Canada studied public attitudes towards multiculturalism and diversity. Two-thirds of respondents said that being a multicultural society was one of the things they liked best about Canada, but the majority of those added the proviso that a "Canadian way of life" must also be preserved. To use Decima's language, Canadians' vision of multiculturalism is "diversity bound by commonality."[4]

While governments made progress in promoting diversity, promoting commonality has been a more difficult task. The decentralized nature of the Canadian federation, combined with well-founded sensitivities about Quebec, the status of aboriginal peoples, and the right of ethnic minorities to preserve their cultural heritage, has meant that there is little consensus about what "promoting commonality" means.

This does not mean, however, that efforts to promote a common Canadian way of life should be abandoned. The Canadian values of democracy, equality, and the rule of law should be nourished and promoted. If I were prime minister, I would direct the Department of Canadian Heritage to work closely with the Council of Ministers of Education in co-ordinating and developing school curricula based on what we used to refer to as "civics": the nature and importance of the Canadian democracy; the rights that Canadians enjoy under the Charter and Canadian statutes; and the responsibilities inherent in citizenship.

I would also direct the Department of Immigration to ensure that new immigrants to Canada were given adequate training in these areas as well. Like official-language training, a sound introduction to Canadian values and the Canadian way of life is an important tool for ensuring integration of new Canadians and the social harmony that would result. This does not mean that immigrants should be encouraged to abandon their cultures, but it does mean that they should know the rights and responsibilities they can expect in their new homeland.

Ensuring Effective Support for Families

It is often said that the Canadian family is in a crisis situation: the rate of family breakdown, domestic violence, the alienation of Canadian youth, and the number of families living in poverty are all a source of great concern.

At the same time, programs that are designed to help families in need are threatened by inefficiency on the one hand and overzealous cost-cutting on the other. And this is taking place when the level of child poverty is unacceptable in a country as prosperous as Canada; when the proportion of elderly citizens is on the increase; and when both the structure and the needs of families are dramatically changing. Providing effective social programs — especially those that have a positive impact on children and youth — may cost a great deal today, but they are an investment in our future. As Judith Maxwell, former president of the Economic Council of Canada, has stated: "If we simply let the programs wither, or limit ourselves to tinkering, our society will polarize into rich and poor, or educated and uneducated.... Governments may spend less on social programs but they will spend a lot more on fighting crime, protecting property and combatting racism. In short, Canada begins to look more like the United States."[5]

This does not mean that we should maintain the *status quo*. With 47 percent of government expenditures going towards social programs, I acknowledge that a reform of social programs in this country is sorely needed. But that social policy review should not merely look at individual programs — such as unemployment insurance, for example — it should look at the whole range of social services and how they are delivered. If I were prime minister, I would expand the social policy review to examine not only those programs currently delivered by the federal government, but also programs like welfare and child care that are in the provincial jurisdiction. I would take a close look at what is working and what is not, and what needs are yet to be fulfilled. What kind of income support is really needed for short-term and long-term unemployment? What kind of support is needed for low-income working parents in order to keep them off the welfare rolls? How should the whole issue of child support be dealt with? What kind of support is needed for aboriginal families, or for families of children with disabilities, or for families who are caring for elderly relatives? What changes are needed in the existing pension regime to adapt to a future in which early retirement, on the one hand, and a trend towards abolishing mandatory retirement, on the other, are transforming the lives of older Canadians?

I cannot provide the answers to these questions, and I realize that most, if not all, of them are being considered by various levels of government. But it is essential that we find out how they fit together and come up with a comprehensive plan for social programs that are effective, efficient, and help those who need them most.

Rationalizing Government and Seeking Out Partnerships

One of the more unfortunate characteristics of the current economic debate is that it tends to see "government" and "the private sector" as mutually exclusive entities, with the main objective being the transfer of activities from the former to the latter. This trend is exacerbated by public cynicism about government and its institutions, about "red tape," bureaucracy, and lack of responsiveness to community concerns.

Merely transferring government functions to the private sector will not automatically make them more responsive or, for that matter, more efficient. An essential component of the policy review process must be to consider what type of structure is most appropriate for each type of service, and to come up with innovative methods of service delivery that transcend the traditional public–private dichotomy.

Developing partnerships and increasing the role of the "third sector" is hardly a new idea. At the municipal level, for example, the use of district health councils and other forms of community-based organizations for service delivery has been around for some time. At the federal level, it is most apparent in aboriginal programs and the devolution of a wide range of health and social services to Indian bands. But this approach may be applicable to a much wider range of areas than has previously been considered.

If we are to reduce the overall cost of government without sacrificing much-needed programs, we should make the development of these types of partnerships a priority. Many functions that are currently handled by government departments may well be better off in the hands of community-based organizations: they could be less expensive, and they will be more responsive. They will also serve to bring Canadians and their governments together, give people a sense of involvement in and responsibility for the services, and eliminate the "them and us" attitude towards governments and the services they provide.

Another way in which government should be rationalized is in the area of law. The oft-repeated comment that Canadians are "the most overgoverned people in the world" is often accompanied by the observation that we have too many laws, and that they are so complex that they are inaccessible to even the most educated average citizen. Just as there must be a comprehensive approach to social services, there must also be a comprehensive approach to law reform.

Take, for example, one area with which I am familiar: restrictions on the promulgation of hate propaganda. Right now, there are references to hate propaganda in the Criminal Code, the Canadian Human Rights Act, the Post Office Act, the Customs Act, the Broadcast Act, and a number of different provincial statutes. Advocacy groups have repeatedly complained that although various government agencies are making an effort to combat hate-mongering, there is little or no co-ordination of these efforts. It is possible that a review of laws related to hate propaganda may result in a consolidation of at least some of those laws, so that a co-ordinated approach to the problem might be more feasible. I suspect that a number of other areas of law could benefit from the same review.

In order to accomplish this goal, I would revive and strengthen the Law Reform Commission and give it the mandate to conduct a comprehensive review of existing federal law. I would also direct it to look into how our laws could be simplified and made more accessible to the general public.

Enhancing Canada's Role in the World

One of the greatest joys of my career has been the opportunity I have had to travel to other countries. Not only have I been enriched personally and professionally by these experiences, but they have given me, to paraphrase the Scottish poet Robert Burns, the ability "to see ourselves as others see us."

You don't have to read the UN's Human Development Report to know that Canada is perceived internationally as one of the world's greatest success stories — a fact that surprises many Canadians, who are preoccupied by our economic woes and our interminable constitutional crises. Canada is a world leader in many fields, from human rights and the conduct of elections to such areas as telecommunications, post-secondary education, and urban planning. We should play to our strengths in the international arena, and invest as much time and effort in sharing our knowledge and expertise as we do in promoting trade in raw materials or manufactured goods. Not only would we be working towards a better world, but we would also reap economic benefits: for business and industry, our universities, and Canadian taxpayers as a whole.

We should also maintain, if not strengthen, our support for multi-lateral organizations, and the United Nations in particular. That support, however, should not be unconditional: as prime minister, I would make United Nations reform a priority. The promise of the UN, which burned so brightly at the time of its founding five decades ago, will not be realized if it continues to be plagued by inefficiency, duplication, and an excessively bureaucratic structure. A united Canada in a united world is perhaps my greatest personal dream, and I still believe that the UN is our best hope of achieving at least the latter.

These are the themes I would pursue if I were prime minister of Canada today. Needless to say, the variations are endless. Let us hope, to again quote Mme. Benoit, that our future will provide Canada with enough "intelligent cooks" to carry them out.

Notes

1. Jehane Benoit, *Encyclopedia of Canadian Cuisine*, 1970.
2. A Decima Research Report to the Canadian Council of Christians and Jews, March 1995, p. 17.
3. Ibid, p. 18.
4. Ibid, p. 8.
5. Judith Maxwell, "It's time to rethink the social role of government," speech to the Canadian Pension and Benefits Conference, June 8, quoted in "Canadian Speeches — Issues of the Day," October 1993.

FIFTEEN

CANADA'S AMBITION FOR UNITY AND PROSPERITY

• • • • • • • • • •
VICTOR L. YOUNG

Born in St. John's, Newfoundland, Victor Young is the chairman and chief executive officer of Fishery Products International Ltd. He is the former chairman and chief executive officer of the Newfoundland and Labrador Hydro Group of Companies and a former special adviser to the premier of Newfoundland. He currently serves as a director on a number of corporate boards, including the Royal Bank of Canada, McCain Foods Ltd., Bell Canada Enterprises, and Churchill Falls Corporation. He holds a master's degree in Business Administration from the University of Western Ontario.

National Ambition as the Standard

WHAT A GREAT HONOUR AND PRIVILEGE IT WOULD BE TO attain the highest political office in our land and to set out on the exciting endeavour of contributing to the economic and social well-being of our nation. Indeed, it has been a real pleasure just to think about the wonderful challenges associated with being prime minister of Canada.

It is my strong belief that Canadians aspire to be a productive and compassionate society, able to achieve a high level of economic, social, and cultural well-being. As prime minister, I would want to build upon these aspirations. My ambition for our country would be to sustain a prosperous and unified Canada through the encouragement of new ideas, the attraction of new investment, the creation of new jobs, and the generation of additional economic wealth. I would consider it my prime responsibility to articulate why each and every policy decision and action of government was consistent with this national ambition for prosperity and unity. It would be the standard against which the success of all government programs would be judged.

As prime minister, therefore, I would strive to establish a broad range of policies all aimed at sustaining a prosperous Canada through the generation of additional economic wealth. It is only through the creation of such economic wealth that our social programs can be saved, our health care and educational systems improved, and our financial position brought under control. A vibrant economy, keeping Canadians on the job, is a prerequisite to maintaining our national spirit and sustaining a prosperous society.

Personal Objective as Prime Minister

As prime minister, my personal objective would be to do everything in my mental and physical power to accentuate the positive; lift the spirits of all Canadians; raise their confidence levels; and keep them moving towards reaching Canada's full potential as the greatest place in the world in which to live, to work, and to enjoy their short time on this earth.

I would concentrate my energies on sending the right signals; setting the proper pace; establishing the right tone; and, most importantly, making things happen in all areas of government activity that are consistent with building a prosperous and unified Canada. Undoubtedly, it would require an enormous amount of discipline to concentrate on making real and positive things happen while not being distracted by the influences of polls, the media, special interest groups, and the pressures of partisan politics. Nevertheless, all of my energies would be focused steadfastly on government actions that would give Canadians a sense of purpose and hope about the future of their country.

Doing the Right Things in the Right Way

I would commit to doing everything in an open manner, with the highest level of integrity, and then let the chips fall where they might in the next election. Simply put, a prime minister must do the right things, in the right way, for the right reasons, for the long-term prosperity of our country.

In dealing with our national ambition, government has to deal with a multiplicity of important issues related to public finance, health care, education, income security, environmental quality, international trade, national security, foreign affairs, and regional disparities. These are the critical issues that cabinet and parliamentary and governmental institutions grapple with on a continual basis. These issues must be fully understood by the prime minister and must occupy an important part of his or her time. But to deal with the complex details of these issues, a prime minister must call upon ministers, caucus, political advisers, and a huge professional bureaucracy. The prime minister's task is to ensure that these issues are always viewed in the larger context of doing the right things in the best long-term interests of the nation.

Championing National Prosperity

My perception of the role and responsibilities of a prime minister may be terribly oversimplified. In my view, however, the prime minister's key role — of championing national prosperity — must be undertaken in its most uncomplicated form. In so doing, he or she can make it clear that there are no special regions, no special provinces, and no special groups of any kind to be accommodated with privileged treatment. In the end, bringing forth creative and innovative government policies aimed at sustaining a prosperous nation for everyone is what will encourage Canadians to feel a sense of unity that is founded on equity, fair treatment, and equal opportunity.

Quebeckers will want to remain in Canada if, and only if, they recognize that it is in their own best interests to do so. Similarly, the best way to do away with the western provinces' sense of alienation or problems of regional disparity is to achieve real success in creating wealth across the country. This creation of economic wealth must be led by the private sector, by large and small businesses, unionized and non-unionized enterprises, in all sectors of the economy. Government's role is to create an environment that gives Canadians the confidence and the pride to work hard for themselves, their families, and their nation. It is the job of the prime minister to nurture that environment so that people stop blaming governments, stop blaming business, stop blaming unions, and start challenging themselves.

The prime minister must set the standard by which all policies and actions will be judged. Each and every government initiative must be put through the rigorous test of whether or not it is in the best interests of sustaining the long-term economic prosperity of the nation as a whole. In these circumstances, the prime minister creates an environment for the country to grow and prosper; for the disparaged regions to become economic contributors to the nation; and for the disgruntled regions to become enthusiastic supporters of our country.

Getting Our Fiscal House in Order

The highest priority in terms of dealing with Canada's long-term prosperity is getting our fiscal house in order. We have failed to do so in the last twenty-five years because successive governments thought they were solving our problems by throwing money at them. Now the money has run out, and we have not only put the present at some risk, we have also placed our future ability to govern a prosperous nation in peril. Reducing the deficit is not about short-term financial issues, it is a long-term prescription to restore Canada's fiscal health so that our children and grandchildren can experience some of the prosperity that present-day Canadians have enjoyed over the years. We can ignore all of this, run away from change, reject financial reality, and spend our way out of short-term problems, but we will have to do this knowing that we have chosen the unthinkable alternative of setting our country on the road to long-term despair.

A crucial part of putting our financial house in order is bringing about a competitive and vibrant economy, which, in turn, must be soundly managed to: 1) pay down our national debt; 2) reduce the burden of taxation on our citizens; and 3) allow the transfer of resources to help the disadvantaged. In other words, those parts of society that are able to create wealth are given the initiative to continue to do so, and those that are disadvantaged are afforded the opportunity to become self-sustaining. This is the exact opposite of the vicious circle of expenditure growth, debt overload, and high taxation within which governments in Canada have been trapped since the early 1970s.

Solving the Poverty Puzzle

Within the context of creating a more competitive economy to generate additional economic wealth, a prime minister must never lose sight of the issue of poverty. We can never claim to be a prosperous country if a significant number of our citizens lives below the poverty line, as is the case in Canada today. Unemployment, illiteracy, social assistance dependence, and despair among Canada's poor all require a national action plan as an integral part of championing prosperity and unity.

I confess to a lack of specifics in tackling this perplexing issue. It is very important, however, that the prime minister be personally accountable for waging an all-out war on poverty. In so doing, it is essential that the wealth created by a growing economy is used effectively to raise the quality of life for those in our society who are most economically disadvantaged. It is the prime minister's job to communicate these values to all Canadians, so that they may understand that there is a moral framework to national policies that transcends the so-called business agenda.

Sending a Wake-up Call to Canadian Youth

As prime minister, I would also want to recognize the special role that the youth of our country will play in the future of Canada. It is the drive and enthusiasm of our youth that will make the Canada of tomorrow greater than the Canada of today. In this regard, a key responsibility of the prime minister is to send out a wake-up call to all young women and men in Canada, telling them that their future and that of our country is, in many ways, in their hands. Thankfully, they will have a great head start on the rest of the world by virtue of being Canadian citizens at the turn of the twenty-first century.

I would want to be perceived not only as the prime minister of Canada for today, but as the prime minister of youth for tomorrow. I would take on the challenge of harnessing the energy generated by the enthusiasm of our youth and champion the issues of staying in school, respecting the individual, celebrating diversity, embracing the age of perpetual technological change, and pursuing happiness in the context of contributing to Canadian society. Trying to encourage our youth to accept these challenges would also keep the prime minister focused on one of the most critical components of a strategy to ensure the long-term prosperity of our nation.

I have a personal comment that might put into perspective my very strong feelings for our country and its youth. In the past few years my business travels have taken me throughout many parts of the United States, as well as to Iceland, Denmark, England, France, Germany,

Japan, Thailand, China, Uganda, Kenya, Russia, and Mexico. Never once in these travels have I had even a passing thought about wanting to live in any of these exciting and fascinating places. Canada is my home. It is the best place on earth to live and to work as we enter the twenty-first century — bar none. If I did nothing else as prime minister, I would want to have contributed significantly to helping our youth recognize the magnificence of this country and had put them on a path towards accepting responsibility for ensuring that Canada maintains its proper place in the new world order of the millennium ahead.

Conclusion

It is so easy, indeed enjoyable, being prime minister on paper. You articulate a national ambition; ensure all government programs are consistent with it; stand up for what you believe in; do the right things in the right way for the right reasons; champion national prosperity and unity; get our fiscal house in order; tackle the poverty crisis; send out a wake-up call to the youth of our nation; and aspire to sustain a prosperous and unified Canada through the encouragement of new ideas, the attraction of new investment, the creation of new jobs, and the generation of additional economic wealth for the nation as a whole.

Is all of this an impossible dream? Can unity and prosperity really be accomplished? In my view, they not only *can* be, they *must* be, if Canada is to survive and thrive in the twenty-first century.

SIXTEEN

DAYS OF OUR LIVES (EXCERPTS FROM THE OFFICIAL "ARMSTRONG MEMOIRS")

• • • • • • • • • •
JOE ARMSTRONG

Joe Armstrong is an author, historian, and heritage publicist. A Toronto resident, he holds a Bachelor of Arts degree from Bishop's University in Quebec. He is a member of the Champlain Society and an honorary member of Le Mouvement Francite. He created and narrated a radio program titled "The Explorer Series" for CBC Radio's Morningside *and served as a cartographic consultant for the film* Black Robe. *His most recently published book is* Farewell the Peaceful Kingdom: The Seduction and Rape of Canada, 1963–1994.

I BECAME CANADA'S TWENTY-FIRST PRIME MINISTER AT 10:02 on the morning of October 9, 1995. It was Thanksgiving Day. The Clerk of the Privy Council, Pierre McIntosh, asked the Governor General, Roméo LeBlanc, that delightful fellow with the two tubby dolphins on his coat of arms, for permission to administer the oath of office to me:

> I, Joseph Charles Woodland Armstrong, do solemnly swear that I will truly and faithfully execute the powers and trusts reposed in me by the People of Canada, so help me God.

And so I became the willing lackey of the people. I made it clear from the start of my campaign in June of 1995 that the country faced galling challenges. Electing this party, the Radical Innovation Party, or RIP, would mean rapid and major relief in the ways Canada was both structured and governed.

We promised to raise living standards and unify the country. We would free the country from its government-imposed values. We would push for freedom. RIP's ideals could be expressed in just one word: freedom.

My address to the nation that evening remains, to this day, the longest fireside chat Canadians have ever been asked to endure....

Selections from Prime Minister Armstrong's Address to the Nation:

Canadian National Youth Service Program

Our government promises great things to the youth of our nation. We will introduce the Canadian National Youth Program — the CNYP — in the spring of 1996. Any high school graduate or university student in Canada will be eligible to apply for a summer job with the national government on an eighteen-month contract. We will maintain 25,000 jobs per annum. The features are as follows:

1. The student enters the CNYP program for sixteen months and must complete it once accepted. If the young person chooses to leave the program before finishing it, he or she will have to reimburse the crown for expenses incurred.
2. Students will participate in four areas: four months of military service, four months' duty in environmental or heritage service, four months' social service, and four months of employment in industry or some other private-sector activity.
3. During the term of the CNYP program, participants will be required to serve in at least two of the six geographic regions of Canada where they do not ordinarily reside: Atlantic Canada, Quebec, Ontario, the Prairies, Pacific Canada, and the North.

Participants from outside Quebec must choose Quebec for at least one of their assignments. Quebeckers must choose at least two of the five geographic regions outside Quebec in which to complete their assignments.

Our intention is clear. We will educate through experience. I will invite the presidents of every Canadian university and college to contribute their ideas of what to include in such a program for credit(s) towards a university degree.

This program will be financed in part by the cancellation of all unemployment insurance benefits for all those less than thirty years of age. Our youth are our most valuable asset. We must treasure them. We must give them the chance to work and to appreciate the freedom to do so.

Taxation and the Economic Burden

During the election campaign, I promised that this government would address the federal deficit and the national debt. At the present rate of expenditure our current national debt of some $650 billion will exceed $1,000 billion by the turn of the century.

In order for Canadians and our industries to compete, individual Canadians and private industry must be freed from the umbilical cord of big government. Therefore, following the Throne Speech and the recall of Parliament on November 15, this government will introduce legislation to reduce taxes and slash the horrendous cost of administering Canada's taxation system. The steps:

1. Beginning in 1996 this government will implement a flat tax at a rate of 25 percent.
2. The Goods and Services Tax (GST) will be phased out over four years.

The Canada First Project

Canadians want to celebrate their heritage. We are an east–west federation. We can only restore the spirit of our country through committing ourselves to one nation dedicated to grand undertakings — to great fun and wonderful adventure.

So I announce here the formation of the Trans-Canada Federation Commission. It will be responsible for constructing a passenger train service that will boast the most advanced technology and the highest speed in the world. Canadians will once again be able to travel easily from the Atlantic to the Pacific by train. The system will be efficient and offer passengers many more points of access. This will be the largest infrastructure investment ever made in North America. It will open on July 1, 2008, the quatercentennial of Samuel de Champlain's landing at Quebec.

If the Brits and the French can dig themselves a Chunnel, then surely Canadians can build a surpassingly powerful economic engine. In the 1960s John Fitzgerald Kennedy called on his fellow Americans to reach for the moon; we Canadians should settle for nothing less than a railway to the stars for the year 2000!

The public and private sectors will finance the project. And we'll do it without increasing our deficit or national debt.

A prime example: today I am announcing the termination of all new commitments to the $6-billion Canada Infrastructure Works program. We can redeploy approximately $3 billion to this effort.

Another large portion of the funding for this national dream will come from the defence budget. Our domestic fight for this federation is the fight of our lives. The government spends some $10 billion of defence's annual $45 to $50 billion in departmental budgets. We will cut defence by $4 billion per annum. At the same time we'll maintain the levels of primary reservists, while reducing regular force personnel from 60,000 to 45,000.[1]

We'll realize more funding, too, thanks to the action taken by the Minister of Defence this afternoon. She has cancelled the defence department's previous capital commitments for armoured personnel carriers and helicopters. The department will lease, and not purchase.

The Public Service of Canada

Two decades ago the English novelist C. P. Snow observed to his Canadian readers:

> You have the finest civil service in the world today. It was based on ours, I know, but it has surpassed it considerably. I suspect most Canadians don't realize it, but it is a fact recognized by civil servants everywhere in the world.

This is no longer so. Our public service is bloated, demoralized, and politicized beyond recognition. There are many reasons for this. The Public Service Commission (PSC) was originally created to protect the Merit Principle and the public interest. Today it protects and serves no one. When did we last hear of a deputy head resigning from the government on a matter of principle?

At the first session of the new Parliament, we will introduce legislation to restructure the Public Service Commission. I have established three principles to revitalize the public service:

1. The Merit Principle shall be the sole and exclusive authority of the Public Service Commission (PSC). Amendments to the Finance Administration Act will ensure that the Treasury Board no longer plays any role in determining merit through setting classification standards. This will eliminate the conflict in law that prevails between the Finance Administration Act and the Public Service Employment Act.
2. Appointments of the Clerk of the Privy Council and all deputy heads shall be subject to public review and to the PSC's own challenge on the basis of merit. The prime minister's appointments to these positions shall be subject to public hearings before a Joint Committee of the Houses of Parliament. The prime minister's unilateral power to make such appointments is suspended.
3. The Imperative Staffing principle is cancelled from now on as set forth by the Treasury Board Secretariat and the Public Service Commission on October 1, 1981. One of those provisions stated:
   (ii) ... the Merit Principle in all bilingual positions has been deferred.

In the substantially downsized federal public service of this government, the bureaucracy shall be capped at 100,000 employees, less than one half the present levels of some 225,000. This restructuring will be complete by July 1, 2000. Canada will need the very best men and women it has in its public life.

On a related note, in its first session of Parliament this government will introduce legislation to wipe out the requirement that public servants must join a union or be members of one.

1. In the last three decades, Canadian federal governments have effectively erased any justification for unions to exist in the bureaucracy. Everyone recognizes, for example, that unions have little or no effect on public service wages, or on the right to strike. This discredits the labour movement as well as the public service.
2. The 1946 decision of Mr. Justice Ivan C. Rand of the Supreme

Court of Canada, which the courts still apply to labour decisions, is archaic and unconstitutional. It requires compulsory union membership on the grounds that non-union workers benefit as much from the bargaining contracts that unions negotiate as union members do. It often forces public servants to finance political activities and implies allegiances that individual public servants may find offensive, such as the endorsement of separatist candidates in the 1993 federal election.

Constitutional Reform: "Constitution 2000"

Section 49 of the Constitution Act, 1982, requires that, within fifteen years from April 17, 1982, the prime minister convene a constitutional conference of the prime minister and the first ministers of the provinces (FMC). Canada's constitution will be subject to formal review by all the provinces in 1997. Canadians will celebrate their new constitution when they celebrate Canada Day, July 1, 2000. This includes its approval by the people.

We must insist on more democracy. Citizens can't be expected to embrace freedom if they have little or no concept of how it works. The fact that there have been only three referendums in Canada's entire history proves this deplorable state of affairs more than anything else.

I want Canadians to enjoy the power of the ballot box, as they so clearly did during the 1992 Referendum on the Charlottetown Accord! During my term of office the following principles will apply:

1. All non-partisan questions will automatically be referred to the Referendum Commission that I have established this afternoon.
2. To have the effect of law, the seven and fifty formula will apply, whereby seven provinces comprising more than 50 percent of the population are required to be in agreement.

During my term of office this government will hold a referendum for the 17.6 million voters to express their wishes on capital punishment and gun control. Their decision will be binding. There will be a national plebiscite on same-sex benefits. There will be another on official bilingualism.[2] As we all know, the people of Canada have never approved either the Charter or official bilingualism in a direct vote.

Senate Reform

Until the results of the Approval Process Referendum in 1998 are in effect, I pledge to you:

> There will be no further prime ministerial appointments to the Senate without each province holding a provincial election to elect these candidates first. The government of Alberta established this precedent in October 1989 when the voters of that province "elected" Stan Waters to the Upper House. The prime minister had to bow to public pressure and, somewhat belatedly, "appoint" Waters to the Senate.

The Supreme Court of Canada

Until the constitution is amended, I will appoint no further justices to the Supreme Court of Canada without a public joint Commons–Senate committee created to review the proposed candidates.

Because this court holds so much power, and because of the Charter embedded in the constitution, I believe Canadians must be much more directly involved in the selection of those who are their nation's ultimate arbiters of justice. This is not the case now.

Electoral Reform and the Canada Constituent Assembly 2000

We can no longer adhere to the injustices of the British first-past-the-post electoral system, saddled as we are with a constitution that has never been tested directly before the Canadian people.

Electoral reform

Before the 1997 constitutional conference, this government will put a referendum to the people of Canada on electoral reform. Today I have asked Patrick Boyer, former MP and expert on such matters, to chair the new Democratic Renewal Commission. I have ordered that the commission's preliminary report be available to Parliament by October 1, 1996. Following a review of it, and before spring 1999, this government will conduct a plebiscite with the people of Canada on those recommendations.

This new electoral commission will be specifically mandated to examine alternative voting methods, such as those used in Germany,

Norway, Switzerland, and Iceland. One of the options to be considered will be the mix-member proportional system (MMP) that many countries in Europe have already adopted.

The Canada Constituent Assembly 2000

The Boyer Commission will also be mandated to recommend a constituent assembly process. The commission's proposal will be put before the people through a direct vote. I envisage a range of options for Canadians to choose from. Therefore, there will be two referendums, the first on process and the second on the results and proposed constitution.

1. The plebiscite on the process alone will be conducted in spring of 1999. It will take recommendations from the 1997 constitutional FMC into account.
2. The second referendum, which will follow the 1997 FMC on the constitution, will be conducted on the proposed new constitution for Canada. It will proceed whether the first ministers reach an agreement or not.

The methodology is simple. Wherever possible, our government will dismantle the trappings of executive federalism *before* the 1997 FMC is held. The people of Canada must endorse this government's proposals overwhelmingly. In contrast to what happened in 1981, no court in the land will be able to ignore the national will — even with the constraints of the amending formulas entrenched in the Constitution Act, 1982.

Term Limits

Even without constitutional reform, this government intends to eliminate incentives for career politician "wannabes." No member of Parliament will be eligible for members' pension benefits for public service for more than three terms in office in the House of Commons, or an aggregate of more than twelve years in public service. The prime minister will be able to make only three exceptions to this rule in any one sitting of Parliament. This is in keeping with the reform and restoration of public service as the sole motivation for people pursuing public office.

The constitution should allow no prime minister to serve for more than two terms in that office, or a period of ten years, whichever is greater. This would be one of the amendments the government would submit to the FMC of 1997. (Of course this will include me!)

Immigration

Canada has always had the most generous immigration policy in the world. We have swung our doors wide open. Over the past few decades this policy has been much abused. Canada has become the laughing-stock for those espousing opportunism, political expediency, greed, and criminal negligence. This will end immediately.

As I have stated many times before, to be a nation a free society must agree on its fundamental elements. Surely immigration is one. We Canadians have not even agreed on what values our constitution should uphold.

This government will introduce legislation that arbitrarily restricts immigration to fifty thousand a year until the turn of the century. Look at the United States: the Immigration and Naturalization Service estimates that more than ten million legal and illegal immigrants will enter that country during the 1990s. On the other hand, fewer than a quarter of a million people have acquired citizenship in Japan since 1945, even through marriage.

For the long term I am satisfied that the national government must substantially reduce its role in the field of immigration. The federal government should set national quotas for its economy and maintain basic requirements of citizenship. In the view of the vast majority of recent immigrants to this nation, this country will become a land of more emigration than immigration.

Aboriginal Government

We will encourage aboriginal self-government. Your government will dismantle the Department of Indian Affairs and turn over its responsibilities to the aboriginal peoples themselves.

However, your government also pledges to ensure that the laws of Canada apply to each and every citizen of the country equally. Therefore, there will be no endorsed, financed, or subsidized levels of government for aboriginal peoples, any more than other Canadians enjoy. We also intend to ensure that the laws of Canada prevail and that the Criminal Code applies to native people as it does to the rest of the population.

Multiculturalism

This department will be closed immediately. The Radical Innovation Party of Canada committed itself to repealing Bill C-93, the Canadian Multiculturalism Act, at its founding convention in 1984.

We believe that the state has no business supporting anything other than the pride and integrity of Canadians in their national culture and citizenship. Canadians have told us loud and clear that state-endorsed and -financed multiculturalism is unacceptable. This message also emerged out of the Citizens' Forum convened under the Mulroney government. A pluralistic society need not endorse its pluralism — or any other "ism."

And now, I'll be happy to take questions from the media.

Allan Fotheringham, *Globe and Mail:* Prime Minister, you've said nothing about the monarchy. In view of the direction Australia's prime minister, Paul Keating, is taking to scrap the Royals, shouldn't Canada consider similar measures?

Armstrong: Allan, as long as I am prime minister, Canada will retain its strong links to the British crown. I believe that we have a choice: we either become a republic similar to the United States, or even a part of it, or we retain our constitutional traditions and have an apolitical head of state. I consider the latter a focal point far superior for our ideals, regardless of who sits on the throne.

Bob MacDonald, *Toronto Star:* During the campaign you said one of your first moves would be to scrap the Charter Challenge program as well as the provision of financing for special interest groups. How do you plan to help minority groups bring their concerns to the attention of government and the public?

Armstrong: I don't. As I have said before, the next federal budget will also include revisions to the Income Tax Act whereby even political contributions will no longer be permitted as a deduction against income or credit towards taxes owing.

Rafe Mair, CBC: What about the CBC? Can you elaborate on your plans?

Armstrong: I am glad you asked that question, Rafe. Previous governments have chosen to strangle the organization rather than deal openly with it and its role. In my opinion the CBC has become irrelevant in the lives of most Canadians.

For many years now, the CBC has either ignored or muffled a whole range of voices in Canada in favour of special interest groups and those with powerful connections to government. Since the 1992 referendum on the Charlottetown Accord, I have seen no change in the corporation's operations to persuade me that the CBC has earned the public's confidence.

I do not agree with some observers that the CBC is either indispensable or a monument to our heritage. Canada doesn't need a silent censor any more than it needs the CRTC with a Telepope to tell us what we can and cannot watch.

In fact, by the year 2000 I intend to close the CBC and invite private broadcasters to fill whatever vacuum they believe that will leave. Maybe there is a role for a state-controlled broadcaster in the more remote regions of the country. This matter will be addressed through public hearings.

In the meantime, I will take whatever legal steps necessary to dismantle the *"deux nations"* structure of CBC that Mr. Mulroney's separatist minister of communications put in place.

Wendy Mesley, *Western Report:* Prime Minister, you have said you will eliminate interprovincial trade barriers within Canada. How do you propose to do this and why? And have you any thoughts on the Free Trade Agreement and NAFTA? You opposed both these pacts.

Armstrong: Wendy, the Canadian Manufacturers' Association estimates that interprovincial trade barriers cost Canadians some $700 to $800 billion every year in waste and inefficiency. If Confederation had one purpose in 1867, it was to wipe out such barriers! It's the "thou shalt not" that the Fathers of Confederation spelled out in section 121 of the British North America Act, which still forms the backbone of our constitution, by the way.

I can now tell you I have set the deadline for the elimination of all interprovincial trade barriers. It will be July 1, 1996. After that day, this government will use the disallowance provision of the constitution — section 90 — to take whatever steps are necessary. No other federation on earth tolerates the nonsense that Canadians do when it comes to moving goods between the provinces.

Which brings me to your final point — the Free Trade Agreement and NAFTA. We're stuck with them and must make them work. But I haven't seen one iota of evidence to suggest that expanding these trading blocs makes sense.

Remember, as a result of the FTA Canada was to gain 400,000 jobs. What did we get? Diddly-squat. But now we're told by some theorists that we gained because we would have lost as many as 800,000 jobs if we *hadn't* entered into free trade with the Americans. I prefer the E. F. Schumacher approach: small is beautiful. But I guess I've been outvoted.

Barbara Amiel, Vancouver *Sun:* Prime Minister, for many months now you have been remarkably quiet about one of your pet peeves: the concentration of the Canadian media. In fact, during the campaign there wasn't a peep from you on it. What's up?

Armstrong: I thought you might be the one to raise that issue, Barbara. But first, welcome back to Canada. We've missed you.

To answer your question: plenty. I want to move immediately on this vital matter. Media concentration in Canada has deepened, worsened considerably since the recommendations of the 1980 Royal Commission on Newspapers were submitted to the Trudeau government. I just happen to have the precise wording right here. According to those recommendations this government will:

1. Strengthen competition or anti-combines legislation;
2. Break up the chains, so that we revert eventually to one newspaper, one owner; and
3. Prevent cross-media ownership.

In their report the commissioners stressed that Canadians would lose a substantial degree of freedom as a result of the "undue concentration of ownership and control of the Canadian daily newspaper industry.... Concentration engulfs daily newspaper publishing."

The government ignored the recommendations completely. But even before the 1980 Royal Commission studied the problem, the 1970 Special Committee on Mass Media — the so-called Davey Committee — identified the same problems! And prior to that, similar, serious concerns were noted by the 1961 O'Leary Commission and duly ignored. You have to wonder, how long does it take?

Whatever the cost, this government will remedy this state of affairs in whatever ways it can. We want to ensure that the constitution guarantees vigorous debate through the media.

I am sure you will agree with me, Barbara, that it's time to act. And of course your husband will agree, *n'est-ce pas*?

Robert Mackenzie, *Alberta Report:* What do you think of the Quebec referendum on sovereignty?

Armstrong: You're a separatist, Bob; you know what I'll do. I'll ignore the vote. After all, as Mr. Justice Robert Lesage of the Quebec Superior Court recently ruled on September 8, 1995, the National Assembly's "ability and power to declare Quebec sovereignty without following the amendment procedures recognized in the Constitution of Canada constitutes a serious threat to the rights and freedoms ... as guaranteed by the Canadian Charter of Rights and Freedoms."

Even if Quebeckers had voted two-thirds in favour of leaving Canada in their own provincial referendum, I as Prime Minister do not accept that some 15 or even 20 percent of Canada's entire population have either the legal or the moral authority to secede.

What else could I possibly do than directly consult all Canadians on such a grave matter? But then, as you know, Robert, I have never accepted the premise that Canada has ever had a national unity crisis. In my view, we have a citizenship crisis and a crisis over values. That's all. And you have heard some of the solutions.

I am absolutely confident Quebeckers will rally to the revitalized Canada that the Radical Innovation Party proposes.

William Thorsell, Montreal *Gazette:* Prime Minister, when will you repeal Bill C-41? Canada's so-called hate law provides harsher penalties for crimes motivated by hate based on race, nationality, colour, religion, sex, age, mental or physical disability, or sexual orientation.

Armstrong: Mighty soon, Bill. This legislation offends the first principle of this government, equality before the law. Repealing this law will be at top of the order paper when Parliament opens on November 15. Of course, there is an alternative — to put this concept before the people in a referendum.

Michael Bate, *Proclivity Press* (Halifax): Throughout your career you have taken a strong stand against special interest groups being given preferential treatment by government. In light of section 15 (2) of the constitution, just how can you stop affirmative-action programs or human rights commissioners, either federal or provincial, from doing just as they please?

Armstrong: I find the equality rights provisions of the Charter contradictory and offensive. First, in section 15 (1), we say that everyone's equal before the law. Then, with section 15 (2), we backpedal and say: "Well, you know, that's really not so. And therefore the state should intervene and fix Mother Nature," in terms of "race, colour, religion, sex, age," etc.

Ours is the constitution of a victim culture. Some of our human rights commissioners remind me of courts of the Spanish Inquisition. I ask you — do we really want tribunals of this nature? Decidedly not. I mean to take whatever action I can at the federal level to diminish the role of these tribunals.

Incidentally, lest we forget, Canada survived magnificently for over a hundred years without what I call the Charter of Fights and Fiefdoms!

Francine Pelletier, CFRB Radio: Did you mean what you said about Canada having an impeachment process whereby the PM can be removed?

Armstrong: I did indeed. During our term of office, I will bring forth legislation by which a prime minister can be removed from office for any of the following: insanity, committing an indictable criminal offence, treason, or showing evidence of critical medical incapacity — or for just disappearing!

I might try to get something like this going for Justices of the Supreme Court of Canada, too. But I'm sure they'll have roadblocks I've never even thought of.

I promise to be the first candidate for consideration, but not till the train service is built.

Susan Delacourt, Toronto *Sun:* During the campaign you totally ignored women's issues.

Armstrong: So what's your point, Susan? My choice of deputy heads and cabinet ministers will show you where I stand. More than half the deputy heads, chosen on merit, are women, and my cabinet includes more women than any other in Canadian history.

Surely my selection of Lise Bissonnette to head up the revitalized Public Service Commission will please some Canadians!

(Next scene: the Post-op Recovery Room at the Ross Memorial Hospital in Lindsay, Ontario)

Nurse Viola: Dr. Lackey, Mr. Armstrong seems to be hallucinating. He's been in here for two hours now, ranting and raving. There's no let-up. He seems to think he's running the country, although I'm not sure what country it is.

Dr. Lackey: Not to worry. Maybe with his bloody gallstones out he'll simmer down now. You sure he's not faking it? This one's had weird dreams as long as I've known him. Who is he today? Winston Churchill or Jacques Parizeau?

Armstrong: Nurse, is it over?

Nurse Viola: You'll be just fine, Prime Minister. Your limousine is waiting to take you to the airport. Dr. Lackey has arranged for a brief convalescence at Stornoway.

Armstrong: He has? Strange. But it won't affect my plans for the Canada Health Act! We're downloading socialized medicine to the provinces — *pronto*. We have no choice. And I remind you, Canada was a very healthy society *before* universal medicare and other socialist programs took us to the brink of bankruptcy....

Notes

1. Projections are based on the main estimates and departmental budgets used for the February 27, 1995, federal budget.

2. Official bilingualism is written into the current constitution. Before directly consulting the people for their mandate in this regard, my government will repeal Bill C-72 within the first session of Parliament. This government considers many of the draconian provisions in this legislation unconstitutional, particularly the powers accorded to the Official Languages Commissioner.

SEVENTEEN

AN EFFICIENT, FAIR, AND SIMPLE INCOME TAX FOR CANADA

• • • • • • • • • •
PIERRE FORTIN

A native of Lévis, Quebec, Pierre Fortin is an economics professor at the University of Quebec at Montreal. He is the current president of the Canadian Economics Association and a research associate with the Economics Growth and Policy Program of the Canadian Institute for Advanced Research. He was recently selected by the Quebec Association of Business Economists (ASDEQ) as the most influential Quebec economist of the last decade. He has been active as an adviser to industry and government. He holds a master's degree in Mathematics from Laval University and a doctorate in Economics from the University of California at Berkeley.

A GOOD TAXATION SYSTEM OUGHT TO BE EFFICIENT, FAIR, simple, and inexpensive to administer. Canada's tax system has instead become inefficient, unfair, complex, and costly. The current tax malaise stems from the fact that the Canadian taxpayers have come to realize it and are expressing their frustration in every way they can. While most recent discussions have focused on the GST, dissatisfaction with the corporate and personal income tax system is also mounting rapidly. Income tax reform is certain to be a major subject of public debate in Canada between now and the year 2000.

Shortcomings of the Current Income Tax System

Our tax system breeds economic *inefficiency*, mainly because our marginal income tax rates, those applicable to the last dollar of income, are very high. In combination with payroll tax and sales tax rates, they generate major distortions in the net economic return of work. For the average Canadian worker, who earns $25,000 annually, a $1 pay increase is first taxed at a rate of about 17 percent on payroll (combining the employer and employee contributions). Federal and provincial income taxation then takes away a further 35 percent of the remaining 83 cents. Finally, the GST and PST bites leave less than 50 cents of true purchasing power. One need not be super-rich in Canada to face a marginal income tax rate in excess of 45 percent; a taxable income of $30,000 is enough. Over 40 percent of taxable income tax returns already exceed that level.

High marginal tax rates have four important negative consequences for economic efficiency. First, they discriminate against effort and productive investment. Second, they encourage the growth of the tax shelter industry, which erodes the tax base and invites further increases in tax rates, and so on in an endless vicious circle. Third, they seriously undermine the international competitiveness of the Canadian economy. Fourth, they encourage tax evasion and the growth of the underground economy. More than an economic problem, our tax quandary has become a moral problem.

This environment leads to the widespread perception that our income tax regime is grossly *unfair*. First, it is much easier for everyone but salaried workers to cheat the system. Evidence on unreported income is, by definition, hard to obtain, but Internal Revenue Service surveys in the United States have consistently shown that evasion is minimal for wages and salaries, and very important for dividends, capital gains, self-employment incomes, and rents and royalties. Second, between two equally qualified persons, the one who displays more ingenuity and energy in exploiting tax shelters comes out richer than the one who simply applies her skills to creating wealth in the economy. In particular, the salaried middle class is frustrated by the fact that the rich can afford the costly legal and accounting services required for maximum exploitation of tax loopholes. Third, on the corporate side, there are widespread disparities in the tax treatment of different types of businesses (small, manufacturing, resource-based, etc.), the sole justification for which lies in history and political clout.

The upshot is that low- and middle-income earners are convinced that the rich do not pay their fair share of income taxes. There are some exaggerations: in 1991, for example, the average income tax rate on incomes exceeding $200,000 was 35 percent, compared with 20 percent for incomes of $30,000. The system does remain progressive. But, given the shelters and the unreported income, it is clearly less progressive than theoretical tax schedules and taxation statistics suggest it is. Moreover, the resulting erosion of the tax base forces increases in rates that, again, fall disproportionately on wage incomes. There is no question that salaried workers have some reason to complain.

Finally, our income tax system has become enormously *complex*. Canadian tax laws, regulations, and jurisprudence already cover tens of thousands of pages. They are growing by the day. A substantial proportion of Revenue Canada employees fail elementary tests of knowledge of the tax system. Even our best tax experts admit they find it very hard to keep up.

The complexity makes the system very costly to comply with and to administer. A recent issue of *Fortune* magazine reported an estimate that puts the total bill for tax record-keeping, audits, filing costs, tax attorneys and accountants, economic distortions, and tax lobbies at more than 8 percent of GNP for the United States. In Canadian magnitudes, that figure would amount to a stunning $60 billion, or just about what the federal government collects annually in personal income taxes. This estimate is possibly too high. But even if the true amount were only one-quarter as large, there would still be very serious cause for concern.

What I have shown so far is that our income tax system has indeed become inefficient, unfair, complex, and costly to manage, and that Canadian taxpayers are right to complain about it. What we need is not more fine-tuning but a fundamental change in our basic approach to the income tax. We need a tax revolution.

In Search of an Alternative System: Basic Principles

How are the objectives we pursue — efficiency, fairness, and simplicity — to be implemented? In thinking about new directions for the income tax, it is useful to begin by setting out two organizing principles.

First, it ought to be recognized that the corporate income tax is nothing but an extension of the personal income tax. It applies to business profits, which are just one particular form of income, accruing to persons who own businesses. The two income taxes, personal and corporate, cannot be treated separately. They must be approached in an integrated manner.

Second, we must distinguish between tax *level* and tax *structure*. The tax level is the total amount of tax revenue governments collect on incomes. The tax structure is the set of rules according to which that given amount of tax revenue is collected. Although we all hope to be paying less tax sometime in the future, the problem we are concerned with here is that of tax structure, not tax level. That is, we are looking for better ways to raise the same amount of income tax revenue as currently.

Given these organizing principles, how are we to bring the tax system back to economic *efficiency*? We have argued that an efficient income tax system should minimize discrimination against work effort and growth-enhancing investment, reduce tax evasion, weaken the underground economy and the tax shelter industry, and restore the international competitiveness of the Canadian tax system. We seek to implement this objective by 1) relying on the lowest possible top marginal tax rate; 2) making it universally applicable on both the personal side and the corporate side; 3) making all business expenditures on plant and equipment, and all personal expenditures on education and training, fully deductible from taxable income in the year of purchase; and 4) allowing businesses with negative taxable income in one year to carry forward the negative tax against future positive taxes.

We also insist on restoring *fairness*. This requires that the new income tax system be clearly progressive, that the amount of unreported non-wage income be reduced, that tax shelters be curtailed, and that disparities of tax treatment across different types of businesses be eliminated. Progressivity means that the amount of income tax paid as a proportion of income (the average tax rate) increases with the level of income. It can be achieved by three means: personal exemptions, rising marginal tax rates, and as few tax deductions as possible for higher-income taxpayers.

But marginal tax rates that increase too much with income levels are no longer acceptable, because they are the main source of economic inefficiency and they encourage tax evasion and the growth of the tax shelter industry, which reduces fairness. We are therefore led instead to compress the difference between the lowest and the highest marginal tax rates. In the first instance, we actually examine the possibility of applying a unique, low, flat-tax rate to both personal and corporate incomes. We choose to achieve fairness by 1) maintaining personal exemptions, and 2) eliminating all tax shelters on the personal as well as the corporate side. Furthermore, a flat-tax rate on business income and the disappearance of tax shelters would effectively end tax discrimination among companies.

Finally, we want to *simplify* the income tax system, and hence reduce administrative and compliance costs. The measures proposed so far already generate a drastically simpler system. On the personal side, this is achieved through the elimination of all shelters, the provision of only a few exemptions (for basic personal needs, family size and structure, age, health status, and employment, education, and training expenses), and the application of either a unique low flat rate or a low top marginal rate. On the corporate side, simplicity also comes from the elimination of shelters and the imposition of the same universal flat rate.

Further simplification would follow from the Hall–Rabushka proposal of a new division of the income tax base between the personal and the corporate levels.[1] In a nutshell, the personal side would tax only wage and private pension incomes (less the personal exemptions), while the corporate side would tax all other incomes (less non-residential business investment). The corporate tax base would be equal to gross revenue from sales, less purchases of goods, services, and materials, less purchases of plant, equipment, and land, and less wages, salaries, and pensions paid out.

Interests, dividends, rental income, royalties, professional income, and other business income would no longer be taxed at the personal level since they would already have been taxed at their business source, where they would be easier to catch. The income bases for the wage and pension tax and the business tax would be very simple to calculate. At the same time, the system would be set up to tax each and every dollar of national income once and only once.

The Flat Tax: Efficient and Simple, but Not Quite Fair

Theory is nice, but it acquires credibility only if it is shown to be workable in practice. Hong Kong is the only industrial country whose income tax system is close to a flat-tax system, combining generous personal exemptions with very few tax shelters. Over the last quarter-century, it has also been one of the fastest-growing economies in the world. While no one pretends that the low-tax system has by itself caused the rapid growth, Hong Kong authorities have always been keen to argue that it has greatly facilitated growth by stimulating investment.

Turning to concrete implications, the first task is to calculate the uniform tax rate that would generate the same aggregate level of income tax revenue as currently exists in Canada. To make the problem operational, I have produced estimates on the basis of taxation and national accounts statistics for the year 1991, the latest year for which detailed data are available. The following table summarizes the results:

TABLE 1

		Billions of $
Gross domestic product		675
Potential gross tax base		557
of which:	Wages and pensions	346
	Business income	211
Less: Deductions and exemptions		228
of which:	Personal exemptions	152
	Business fixed investment	76
Equals: Potential net tax base		329
of which:	Taxable wages and pensions	194
	Taxable business income	135
"Realistic" net tax base		329
of which:	Taxable wages and pensions	214
	Taxable business income	115
Target income tax revenue		109
achieved by:	Wage and pension tax	71
	Business tax	38
Required uniform tax rate		33 %
of which:	Federal tax rate	21 %
	Average provincial tax rate	12 %

This table estimates that the largest possible gross income tax base before exemptions in 1991 was $557 billion (of which about $346 billion came from wages and private pensions, and $211 billion from other types of income).[2] Next, the concrete example of flat income tax worked out in the table assumes that personal exemptions would be $152 billion. This figure is equal to the total amount of personal exemptions that were used as the basis for non-refundable tax credits in 1991 ($163 billion), less the deductions for unemployment insurance (UI) premiums ($5 billion) and Canada Pension Plan/Quebec Pension Plan (CPP/QPP) contributions ($6 billion), which would be abolished. Furthermore, the national accounts report that non-residential business fixed investment was $76 billion in 1991. Crediting these two items against the potential gross tax base yields a potential net base of $329 billion.

I would then introduce two basically offsetting adjustments to arrive at a more "realistic" tax base: 1) some $20 billion of personal exemptions were not actually used by taxpayers whose income was too small to be taxed; 2) even if the new tax system is able to reduce tax evasion, some business income, perhaps about $20 billion also, will remain unreported. These adjustments leave the "realistic" tax base unchanged at $329 billion.

Finally, in 1991 Ottawa and the provinces together collected $109 billion of income tax revenue (of which $94 billion came from the personal tax and $15 billion from the corporate tax). Since $109 billion is 33 percent of the $329 billion tax base, 33 percent turns out to be the uniform tax rate which could have generated exactly this much revenue. The 1991 sharing of total income tax revenue between the two levels of government would have required leaving 21 tax points to Ottawa and sending 12 points to the provinces. The distribution of tax revenue among provinces would, of course, have reflected the various provincial tax codes of 1991. Ontario and Quebec would have obtained more, and Alberta and British Columbia less, than the national average.

The basic result here is that a flat tax applicable to the largest possible income base, subject to the *same* aggregate level of personal exemptions as currently and to full deductibility of business investment, would lower the top marginal tax rate to 33 percent from a level now in excess of 50 percent in every province except Alberta (where it is 46 percent). For the federal income tax alone, the reduction would be from the current 32 percent to 21 percent.

This low flat-tax system achieves the efficiency and simplicity goals we are pursuing. But it does not meet our standard of fairness, for two reasons. First, in all provinces the total marginal tax rate currently applicable to low- and middle-income taxpayers lies *below* the flat tax rate of 33 percent: it ranges between 26 percent in Alberta and British Columbia and 31 percent in Quebec, with a median of 28 percent. Second, the new system would deprive this modest-income group of the deductions and tax credits arising from five important sources: registered pension plans (RPPs), registered retirement savings plans (RRSPs), union dues, unemployment insurance (UI) premiums, and Canada or Quebec Pension Plan (CPP/QPP) contributions.

Figure 1 compares the 1991 federal tax under the current and flat-tax regimes for individuals who had nothing but wage income to report, which is the case for the vast majority of taxpayers. It is assumed that under the current system the individual gets her basic personal credit and

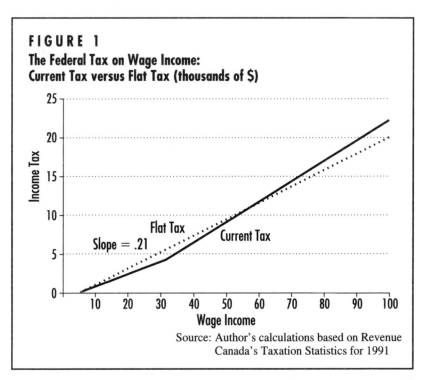

FIGURE 1
The Federal Tax on Wage Income:
Current Tax versus Flat Tax (thousands of $)

Source: Author's calculations based on Revenue
Canada's Taxation Statistics for 1991

her UI and CPP/QPP credits. She claims deductions for her RPP, her RRSP, and her union dues equal to the average of her income group. Under the flat tax, she gets only the personal exemption ($6,280 in 1991).

It can immediately be seen that the flat tax puts wage-earners with incomes below $65,000 at a disadvantage. Low- to middle-wage earners have to pay roughly 30 percent more federal taxes than under the current system. A similar conclusion holds for the total federal and provincial income tax, since everywhere except in Quebec the provincial tax is a multiple of the federal tax. The disadvantage for low- and middle-income groups would be smallest in Quebec because the lowest marginal tax rate there (31 percent) is already the highest in the country under the current regime.

Restoring Fairness: A Compromise Two-tier System

The flat-tax system we have just considered would be efficient and simple, but it would not be perceived as fair. The natural question is then whether there exists another flat-tax system that would be fair in the sense that no worker earning less than $30,000 would pay more taxes than in the current system.

The answer is yes, but this objective could be achieved only at the cost of increasing the flat-tax rate to an absurd level, contradicting efficiency. Operationally, we would have to shift the flat-tax line of Figure 1 to the right towards a more generous personal exemption level, and then make the line steeper so as to generate more revenue per taxed dollar and keep total tax revenue from the wage and business income taxes on net unchanged at $109 billion. But such a system would raise the personal exemption to $20,000 and the flat-tax rate to 36 percent at the federal level alone and to 56 percent for the two levels of government combined. This flat universal rate would exceed even the current top marginal rate, an absurd situation which would contradict the efficiency goal we are seeking to achieve.

Consequently, a compromise must be struck between the objectives of efficiency and fairness. One reasonable approach would be to raise the basic personal exemption to $8,000 (to replace the loss of popular deductions and tax credits), keep the federal marginal tax rate at 17 percent for wage incomes up to $30,000, and set it at 24 percent for earning levels above $30,000 and for business incomes. Including the provincial tax, the two marginal rates would be 26 and 37 percent. This compromise two-tier system would achieve the $109-billion revenue target, the top marginal tax rate would still decline substantially, and no pure wage-earner would pay more taxes than under the current system. The proposed two-tier system and the current regime are compared in Figure 2.

One conspicuous characteristic of the two-tier wage tax is that it would reduce the taxes on earnings in excess of $30,000. Figure 2 shows that the federal tax break would increase from about $100 on a $45,000 wage to over $2,000 on a $100,000 wage. Would this mean that the rich would actually pay less in taxes? The answer is no. The main reason is that they would lose the tax shelters on their *non-wage* incomes. They would also be negatively affected by two other developments: taxing business income at its source would reduce evasion, and the new system would depress the after-tax interest rate, and hence many forms of investment income.

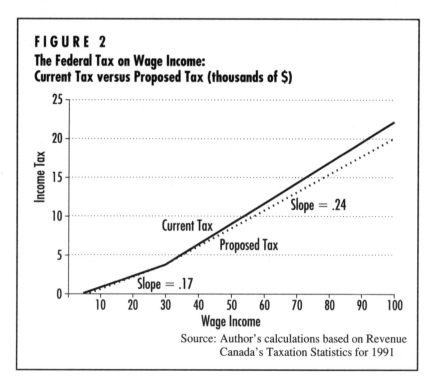

FIGURE 2
The Federal Tax on Wage Income:
Current Tax versus Proposed Tax (thousands of $)

Source: Author's calculations based on Revenue
Canada's Taxation Statistics for 1991

Taxation statistics show that non-wage income is concentrated among high-income taxpayers. In 1991, 18 percent of all taxpayers reported total incomes of $40,000 or more. They received 46 percent of interest income, 80 percent of dividend income, and 89 percent of taxable capital gains. Tax shelters affecting non-wage income are key to understanding why, rather startlingly, the alternative income tax system just explained would be more, not less, progressive than the current system, despite the substantial reduction in the top marginal rate.

To get a flavour of what the elimination of tax shelters on non-wage income does, consider a taxpayer whose total assessed income was $100,000 in 1991. Taxation statistics show that she was typically earning $75,000 in salary and $25,000 in non-wage income. She was claiming $15,000 of deductions, $2,000 of non-refundable tax credits, and a $1,700 dividend tax credit. In the average province, she had to pay $27,000 in total (federal and provincial) income taxes.

In our two-tier system, her personal exemptions would usually amount to $10,000. This includes the new $8,000 basic personal exemption and $2,000 more from other personal and family exemptions claimed on average in her income category. Combining the wage tax on her salary and the business tax on her non-wage income,[3] total income taxes on her $90,000 assessed taxable income would have increased to $30,000, or $3,000 more than under the current system. Taxes on wage income would fall, but taxes on non-wage income would rise, making the system more progressive on net.

Eliminating Tax Credits and Deductions and Fostering Growth

In the proposed system, all credits and deductions are to be eliminated from the wage tax, except the basic personal exemption, exemptions for family size and structure, age and health status, and deductions for employment, education, and training expenses. Gone will be the deductions for RPPs, RRSPs, and union dues. Private and public fringe benefits (including UI premiums and CPP/QPP contributions) will be taxed fully, the employee portion by the wage tax and the employer portion by the business tax. Interest, dividends, and net capital gains will also be taxed fully, all at the business level. These radical changes will likely be met with fierce resistance by special-interest tax lobbies. This will put the political feasibility of the proposed system to a severe political test.[4] What can be said in its support?

The elimination of tax credits and deductions is the most critical element of the whole operation because it is the main channel through which the income tax base can be widened and the tax rate reduced. There lies its rationale. A vote for keeping some or all tax credits and deductions is a vote against lower marginal tax rates, against simplicity, and for the prevalence of private interests over the general welfare of society.

UI premiums, CPP/QPP contributions, health and safety premiums, etc., are portions of labour compensation spent on insurance against unemployment, old age, illness, work accidents, and so on. They are just special forms of taxable income, and there is no logic in treating them otherwise. We are taking a similar view of the deduction for union dues, which are income spent on the services of labour unions. It is noteworthy that the deduction for union dues benefits high-income taxpayers more than low-income taxpayers: in 1991, 73 percent of the total amount claimed for this item came from the richest 30 percent of taxpayers. If the concern is just that withdrawing the credits for UI premiums and CPP/QPP contributions and the deduction for union dues will hurt low- and middle-wage earners, then the natural solution is exactly the one we are proposing: replace them with a universal increase in the basic personal exemption.

In the current tax system, interest paid is fully deductible from corporate income while dividends are fully taxed. A partial offset is that interest income is fully taxed at the personal level while dividend income is subject to partial deduction. By imposing the same standard business tax rate on interest and dividends, the new system puts an end to what remains of tax discrimination against dividends relative to interests, which discourages entrepreneurial effort and encourages business financing based on debt instead of equity. Including interest paid on loans and dividends paid on equity fully into taxable business income does not increase the financial burden on businesses, because interest and dividend income are no longer to be taxed at the personal level. What will happen is that instead of making high (before-tax) interest and dividend payments, as they currently do, businesses will make low (after-tax) interest and dividend payments.

The case of capital gains is very similar. In the new tax system, the taxation of capital gains arises naturally through the full deduction of the purchase price of business assets and the inclusion of their sales price into the tax base upon disposal. Capital gains taxation at the personal level disappears because it would here again amount to double taxation.

With the proposed changes to the tax system, the RRSP credit as we know it today would be eliminated. However, the new system would cleverly allow *all* private savings to be invested in a single, economy-wide RRSP. How is this possible, given that the new wage tax allows no deduction or credit for personal savings? The answer is that when personal savings find their way into a business firm to finance a fixed investment (whether as a direct loan or purchase of equity by the saver, or through some financial intermediary), they are deducted fully from the taxable income of the firm, and hence of the person who ultimately holds the claim. In other words, just as in the case of RRSPs, the money you save works for before-tax returns and the double taxation of savings is avoided. In the end, you get the same tax-exempt interest or dividend as under the current RRSP scheme.

The new scheme is wider in scope, because it gets rid of existing RRSP annual ceilings. It is also more dynamic because savings are tax-deductible if, and only if, they really work to promote domestic economic growth through the mechanism of full first-year depreciation of business investment. "Rentier" firms pay more taxes; growing firms pay less. Contrary to the RRSP regime, the new system imposes no administrative cost whatsoever on taxpayers, financial institutions, or Revenue Canada. Finally, it does not distort rates of return wildly, as today's RRSPs can do.

To see this, assume you put $2 this year into a RRSP, your true out-of-pocket cost being only $1 given the RRSP deduction at a 50 percent marginal income tax rate. If the market rate of return is 10 percent, you draw $2.20 from your investment next year. But if meanwhile your income has fallen substantially and your marginal tax rate has declined to 40 percent, you will pay 88¢ of income tax on your $2.20 and be left with an after-tax amount of $1.32. The true final return on your initial dollar of saving will therefore be 32 percent. This is a wild, purely tax-related distortion of the return on RRSP saving. The new system does away with this anomaly because the saving is deductible from taxable business income at the marginal rate of 37 percent when it is financing a business investment, and the interest or dividend income it generates is taxed at exactly the same business tax rate of 37 percent when it is paid out. No distortion of the rate of return by the tax system is possible any more.

Conclusion

Our current income tax system has become inefficient, unfair, and complex. Canadian taxpayers have come to realize it, and they are asking for a sensible, practical alternative.

To summarize, the new system I propose has four characteristics: 1) it provides strong investment incentives; 2) it is more progressive than the current system; 3) it lowers the top marginal tax rate substantially while procuring the same amount of tax revenue as presently; and 4) it is an extremely simple system. Many will argue that this is a radical proposal. But this is exactly the point. Radical change is what we now need to achieve what Canadian taxpayers are longing for all across the political spectrum: a return to efficiency, fairness, and simplicity.

This is not the only task ahead. Not only do we have to turn our income tax system around, but we also ought to make sure that, once reformed, the new system is not going to drift again towards inefficiency, inequity, and complexity in the future. This requires that we look into ways of reorganizing our democratic institutions so as to prevent the tax shelter industry from beginning to erode the income tax base again and forcing a return to the "wonderful world" of high marginal tax rates.

Tax lobbies are polluters of the tax environment. They reap large benefits from their egotistic and myopic individual action in favour of special interest groups. But, by so doing, they collectively impose on the rest of society the substantial costs of rising marginal rates, rising inequity, and rising complexity. We will have to think hard about means of protecting our democracy from tax pollution, just as we protect our world from environmental pollution.

Notes

1. Robert E. Hall and Alvin Rabushka, *The Flat Tax*, 2nd edition (Stanford: Hoover Institution, 1995). My own interest in the flat tax goes back to 1982: Pierre Fortin, "L'impôt en un tour de main," *Le magazine Affaires*, Montreal, November 1982.

2. This is equal to gross domestic product (GDP), less indirect taxes net of subsidies, and less imputed items amounting to 5.6 percent of GDP.

3. The non-wage income she receives is now *after-tax* income because it has already been taxed at 37 percent at the business level. This business tax is true income tax that has to be added to the wage tax she pays.

4. In this debate, Canada happens to be better positioned than the United States: very fortunately, we do not need to abolish the mortgage interest deduction because we do not have one. By creating a vicious incentive to channel too much savings into owner-occupied housing instead of business investment, this tax measure is operating as an important drag on American economic growth.

EIGHTEEN

IF I WERE THE
PRIME MINISTER

• • • • • • • • • •
NANCY GREENE RAINE

*N*ancy Greene Raine is a former Olympic and world ski champion, having won gold and silver medals for Canada at the 1968 Olympic Games. She was the winner of the 1967 and 1968 World Cup of Skiing. In addition, she was a six-time Canadian champion. Nancy is a public speaker and television commentator as well as the co-owner of a condominium lodge in British Columbia. The former recipient of the Lou Marsh Trophy in 1967 and 1968 as Canadian Athlete of the Year, she was named British Columbia's Female Athlete of the Century and an Officer of the Order of Canada.

IN CANADA TODAY, THE PRIME MINISTER HAS MORE POWER than most Canadians realize. He chooses the cabinet. He can ask any minister to resign, and if the minister were to refuse, the prime minister could ask the governor general to remove him. Cabinet decisions are not necessarily taken by majority vote, and if most, or even all, of the cabinet were opposed to his view, a strong prime minister could simply announce that his view is the policy of the government. Unless his dissenting colleagues are prepared to resign, they must bow to his decision. The Canadian prime minister has enough power under our constitution to provide strong leadership and to implement change. The only true check on the prime minister's power is that our constitution compels him to call an election at least every five years.

If I were the prime minister, I would have been elected on a clear and unequivocal platform of reform. I would have promoted my philosophy, my values, and my proposals for change during the election campaign. There would be no surprises or hidden agendas.

I believe that individual responsibility is the cornerstone of an independent democracy, and I believe that a country where citizens give up their responsibility to look after themselves is a country that is enslaved.

I believe that most of the social and economic problems Canada is facing today have come as a result of successive governments running deficits and piling up the national debt, to the point where it is now at a crisis level. Our national debt stood at an estimated $544 billion on March 31, 1995, and in April, when Moody's Investors Services downgraded Canada's credit rating for the first time ever, one of their analysts said: "Canadians have only just begun to see the full effects of the kind of austerity that's needed to stabilize the situation."[1]

Besides an economic crisis, Canada also has a crisis of values. As our country has become more and more socialistic over the past thirty years, we have gone from being a nation of strong, independent people with a solid work ethic and high degree of self-reliance to a society where a significant number of people feel it is their right to be looked after.

If I were the prime minister, I would promote a philosophy of self-responsibility and independence. I would promote the old-fashioned values of thrift and saving, and stop measuring our standard of living by financial benchmarks. I would promote seeking a quality of life that comes with personal financial security and solid family values.

Abraham Lincoln made the following statements, which still hold true today:

You cannot bring about prosperity by discouraging thrift.
You cannot strengthen the weak by weakening the strong.
You cannot help the wage-earner by pulling down the wage-payer.
You cannot further the brotherhood of man by encouraging class hatred.
You cannot keep out of trouble by spending more than you earn.
You cannot build character and courage by taking away man's initiative and independence.
You cannot help men permanently by doing what they could and should do for themselves.

I agree with him completely.

We live in one of the most blessed countries in the world, with an abundance of natural resources and a healthy and educated population. We benefit from a rich heritage that comes from a wide variety of cultures. There is absolutely no reason why we should not be able to pull ourselves out of our present economic troubles and live up to our personal and national potential.

Solving our fiscal problems won't be easy, and it will require sacrifice from everyone, but it is possible. If we balance the budget and begin to pay down the debt, capital investment will flow into Canada, fuelling a new prosperity.

Socialism, the Deficit, and the Debt

With the economic failure of communism and socialism in the Eastern Bloc countries, many Canadians have begun to question our own level of socialism. While Canada has never elected a socialist government federally, there is no doubt that the NDP, and the CCF before it, influenced successive Liberal and Conservative governments to introduce many socialist programs. While many of these programs were easy to justify, it is doubtful that their long-term impact on Canadian society was recognized at the time of implementation.

In the 1960s, business was booming, jobs were plentiful, and Canadians young and old were confident that our country was the best place in the world. As "Trudeaumania" swept the country, we had a vision of a just society, and one that was compassionate and caring. Unfortunately, the programs we've put into place in the last thirty years have not resulted in a just society, and there seems to be less and less compassion and more and more people in need.

It is now virtually impossible to raise a family on one person's income — which was the norm twenty-five years ago. Today few people are sure of the future. Young people have difficulty finding jobs; older people can't seem to get ahead, and they worry about the future for their children and grandchildren.

The typical Canadian family is being attacked on all sides. It used to be normal to get married, have a family, buy a home, and basically stay married and live happily ever after. Men and women became couples. Today, too often they become combatants. We have rising divorce rates, dysfunctional families with physical and sexual abuse, wife-beating, husband-bashing, and abused or problem children.

A vicious circle has evolved. As Canadians pay more and more taxes, there are more and more demands for social services — everything from "free" health care to unemployment insurance and pensions. And the more government tries to deliver, the more our deficit, debt, and taxes go up.

We ask our government to deliver programs for all kinds of special needs and interests, from the disabled and women's programs to multiculturalism and employment equity. For every perceived need, there is an interest group applying pressure for government funding — the arts, culture, sports, recreation, the list goes on and on. Using money taxed from working Canadians to pay for special interest programs may have been justifiable when our budget was in a surplus, but when we are borrowing from our grandchildren, it is unconscionable.

The list of programs and services is long, but few if any can be delivered more economically by government than by the competitive free market. It is time that we recognize that governments have taken on more than we can afford. The reality is that many of Canada's social programs are not only unnecessary, they are often a disincentive for individuals to become responsible for themselves.

If I were prime minister, I would move quickly to institute a program of fiscal reform. I would use every method possible to communicate to Canadians not only the seriousness of our financial situation, but exactly what must be done for recovery. I would take a lesson from Ross Perrot in presenting the economy with flip-charts and graphics so that every Canadian, regardless of education or experience, could understand what lies ahead. I would be tough and I would probably be very unpopular, but I would not falter in changing and reforming the way our government deals with the economy.

Downsizing Government

With the Reform Party promoting fiscal responsibility, and with the U.S. government attempting to balance its budget, Canadians are finally beginning to understand the problems we face. Awareness has never been higher that we need to make fundamental changes to the way our government works, and many top business consultants are turning their attention to the management of governments. As consultant Peter Drucker has said, "Every agency, every policy, every program, every activity, should be confronted with these questions: 'What is your mission?' 'Is it still the right mission?' 'Is it still worth doing?' 'If we were not doing this, would we go into it now?'"

We must rethink and revitalize government. We need to go beyond "reinventing" government (doing things better and more cheaply) and actually "deinvent" it. We must go through all government programs and add one final question to Mr. Drucker's list: "Is it morally justifiable for us to have this program paid for by our grandchildren?"

As Lincoln said, *"You cannot help men permanently by doing what they could and should do for themselves."*

If I were prime minister, I would implement spending cuts in the following five ways:

1. A smaller government

I would start by cutting the number of ministers, secretaries of state, and parliamentary secretaries. All facets of government would have their operating budgets trimmed, especially the Senate, which would either be reformed or abolished. Perhaps most importantly, I would immediately set an example by reforming the pension plans of politicians and senior civil servants to bring them into line with those in the private sector. I believe before asking Canadians to take cutbacks, politicians must take them first.

2. Decentralize and privatize

I would work with the provinces and territories to have programs and services delivered and funded by the most effective and efficient level of government. Where changes were made, the appropriate share of tax dollars would be taxed directly by the provinces. In decentralizing, I would maintain national standards in areas that affected the public's health and safety. I would privatize as many services as possible and sell off government assets wherever it made sense. I would look at the experiences of other countries and, while not holding a fire sale, would move inexorably towards a truly downsized government.

3. Eliminate grants and subsidies

I would immediately reduce and eliminate all regional development programs and subsidies to business. Not only are these programs costly, they distort the natural workings of a free enterprise system. It has been estimated that the government could save $4.7 billion by eliminating these programs, without affecting individual Canadians.[2] I would set out a five-year program to reduce and eliminate grants and subsidies to cultural organizations, the arts, sports, and other non-essential programs. (I'm sure Canadians would still find a way to support symphony orchestras and national teams.) At the same time, however, I would continue with transfer payments to guarantee that individuals in the poorest provinces have access to services equivalent to the Canadian average.

4. Means tests for entitlements

I recognize that if we are to balance our budget, we must decrease spending on social programs. I would target assistance to those who really need it, and would introduce means tests for all entitlement programs. Currently, federal pension payments amounting to $10 billion go to households with an income greater than the national average of $54,000.[3] Payments for the Canada Pension Plan, Old Age Security, and Guaranteed Income Supplement are not secured by investments but come from the general operating budget, and costs are projected to escalate as the population ages. I would expose the weakness of our current pension situation and provide more incentives for individuals to establish their own RRSPs. I would also change the unemployment insurance program so that it became an actuarially sound insurance program for employees who seek income security. Seasonal employees would be required to save for their anticipated down-time.

5. Downsize the bureaucracy

As government services were downsized, I would see that the bureaucracy was downsized as well. I would ensure that federal government jobs are paid relative to the cost of living where they are located, and in no case would the government pay rates exceed those of the private sector. Canada has an excellent public service with many talented and hard-working employees; however, when their pay scale and benefits are out of sync with those of the private sector it creates ill-will on the part of equally hard-working and over-taxed Canadians.

Government and politics are not like business, which operates with the reality and discipline of the bottom line. Public sector managers face obstacles that would never exist in private business. It is very difficult and expensive for them to downsize their staff, and even if they do, the work-load continues. They cannot opt out of serving their customers, and they operate in a stifling maze of rules and regulations, all designed to protect the public purse. To downsize government won't be easy, but if we want to save medicare and old age pensions, we will have to cut all other programs that are not essential.

Before making program-cutting decisions, I would need to know exactly what the programs and policies were costing, and this is very difficult to determine under the current government accounting procedures. I would adopt private sector budget methods, such as accrual accounting, to reveal just how much policies cost. I would recognize also that for the public to endure the hardships that will come with my hard-nosed cost-cutting they must be convinced that the cuts are necessary, and they must be able to see that progress is being made. I would ask the auditor general to produce quarterly reports, not just on government waste, but on its progress to eliminate the waste.

Most of these proposals for cost-cutting are not new, but if I were prime minister and had been elected on a platform of balancing the budget and eliminating the debt, I would move much more aggressively than the current government is doing.

New Zealand has proven that the faster the change in direction is made, the faster new investment flows into the country. As Ralph Klein has said, "You can't leap a chasm in two jumps."

Deregulation and Cutting Red Tape

Free trade and the GATT have created a very competitive market for Canadian businesses. Any unnecessary restrictions on the ability of businesses to operate efficiently and to react quickly to market forces will inhibit the economic growth that is needed for Canada to overcome its deficit problems. It is more important than ever to use every possible means to minimize government red tape.

While there are important roles for government to play in regulating certain aspects of business, there is probably no justification for the implementation of regulations that are restrictions to the free market. If I were prime minister, I would institute a review of all regulations, asking once more some key questions: "Is this regulation really necessary?"

"Will Canadian products lose their competitive edge with this regulation?" "Is this regulation cost-efficient?" "Is the cost of enforcing the regulation worth it?" "If we did not have this regulation already in place, would there be a demand for it in today's reality?"

As Lincoln said, *"You cannot help the wage-earner by pulling down the wage-payer."*

Taxation Reform

While implementing major spending cuts and accelerating privatization and deregulation, I would put into place a taxation system with incentives for Canadians to become self-reliant and productive.

Over the years, our system of taxation has become incredibly complex, to the point where our existing Income Tax Act is over 1,400 pages long. I would commission the development of a completely new taxation system. I would insist that it be simple enough so that most Canadians would not need an accountant to calculate their taxes.

As prime minister, I would promote a simple income tax formula with, for example, the first $12,000 earned being tax free, after which there would be a flat 25 percent rate on total income earned, including capital gains. An additional tax-free allowance would be given for families with children, $5,000 each for dependants and non-working spouse to recognize the value to society of a family raising their own children. In the case of a divorce, an option would be given as to which parent declared the $5,000 deduction allowance, taken into consideration at the time of settlement. There would be no extra deduction for couples without children.

The only additional exemption, limited to 10 percent of total income, would be for charitable donations, recognizing that as the government moves away from providing social services, charitable organizations will be more important than ever.

The capital gains tax exemption would be done away with because it favours the wealthy; however, a flat 25 percent tax rate would be an incentive for the accumulation of wealth. Inheritance taxes would also be a flat 25 percent payable over a period of years based on the amount inherited.

To attract international capital, Canada's corporate tax rates must be competitive on a world basis. Again, I would propose a flat rate of 25 percent on corporate profits. Allowable expenses would be reviewed, and only legitimate business expenses would be accepted. Depreciation allowances would be reduced, with the eventual target of eliminating this as a tax write-off in favour of a much lower tax rate on profits. International investment seeks out low tax rates, with rates between 15 percent and 25 percent common in Southeast Asia. In Canada, corporations with profits above $2 million pay 54 percent of their total profits in taxes. Is it any wonder that new investment in Canada is drying up!

Federal and provincial sales taxes would be rationalized and collected in an efficient and cost-effective way. As prime minister I would implement a 10 percent tax on all goods and services, with absolutely no exceptions or exemptions. The GST revenue would be split between the various levels of government, with 4 percent going to the federal government, 4 percent to the provincial governments, and 2 percent shared by the municipal or regional jurisdiction where the tax is collected.

The new GST would be collected at every level of production and distribution as at present but all businesses would be included. It is very important that the consumption tax (GST) be shared at all levels of government. A goods and services tax encourages thrift and savings as you only pay tax on what you spend.

To encourage private retirement savings, I would change the legislation to bring the tax-deductibility of annual contributions to RRSPs up to the same level as other pension plans. Canadians need a real incentive to plan to save for their own future security, especially since government pensions are underfunded and at risk.

As prime minister I would reform the tax system to provide rewards and incentives for productive, working Canadians and to encourage thrift and personal saving.

As Lincoln said, *"You cannot bring about prosperity by discouraging thrift."*

Values, Rights, and Responsibilities

Two thoughts keep running through my mind: one, that the measuring of our standard of living should be value-driven, and not related to income or purchasing power; and two, that the growth in government programs has resulted in less freedom for individuals to be responsible for their own decisions and actions.

Standard-of-living statistics do not tell the full story of many Canadians' quality of life. There is a vast difference between the cost of living in a city and of living in a rural area. Though the rural family income may be below the poverty line, a family with a garden and access to hunting and fishing can have a good quality of life. If you add the value of a strong family with a solid work ethic, the security of life in the country is often much higher than that of the family in the city, mortgaged to the hilt and worried about crime, drugs, and other stresses.

People must assume responsibility for their actions. Those who break the law must serve sentences appropriate to the crimes they have committed. Where a crime involves property, retribution should be made, and for crimes of violence, including drug trafficking, full sentences should be served, and in spartan conditions. Convicted felons should lose the right to vote while they are serving their sentences. Finally, if I were prime minister, I would immediately implement a sexual predator law to protect society from dangerous sexual offenders.

Recently it has become more and more common to sue for liability when, logically, the persons suing should have known they were exposing themselves to risk. As prime minister, I would change the law to limit liability and clarify the responsibilities of individuals in order to reduce frivolous lawsuits. Not only do these lawsuits place a burden on our courts, but the fear of them is tying up our regulatory agencies, and bureaucracies are growing to enforce more and more regulations just to protect public agencies from being sued. This trend must be changed. People must accept responsibility for their own actions.

On the other hand, sometimes people want to accept risk, and the government's regulations will not permit it. I believe people should have the freedom to accept the consequences of their own actions.

For example, Canadians should have the right to seek alternative medical treatments (and alternative practitioners should have the right to practise). Canadians should also have the right to seek medical services in private clinics, and to pay for them. There is something repugnant about a system that rations access to health care while at the same time denying citizens the right to purchase medical services in their own country. If I were prime minister, I would give the provinces the freedom to deliver health care services in the way that best suits their needs. I would institute a list of basic services that would have to be delivered to all Canadians regardless of their ability to pay, but I would allow each province to address the problem of health care costs as they choose. I would encourage provinces to exchange experiences, expecting that a new, distinctly Canadian health service would evolve.

It is frustrating for hard-working and frugal Canadians to compare their modest lifestyle with what appear to be the overly generous benefits going to people who do not work. No one should expect that it is his or her right to get something for nothing. Social programs must be designed to provide short-term assistance to those in need, and to provide individuals and families with the incentive and the ability to take responsibility for themselves. Our educational institutions should be challenged to ensure that young persons, no matter whether they are academically inclined or not, are trained and qualified for a job when they leave school.

If I were prime minister, I would create awareness that taking assistance from the government is really taking money from working people. I would make it socially undesirable to seek assistance from the government.

As Abraham Lincoln said, *"You cannot strengthen the weak by weakening the strong."*

National Unity

If I were prime minister, while focusing on implementing major change in the financial side of government, I would also provide strong leadership in the matter of national unity.

I believe that the government must be very careful not to put the interests of any one group of Canadians ahead of those of another. The fastest way to divide a country is to treat one group of people differently from another — and if that group is a visible minority it can easily result in their becoming a target of racial discrimination.

With cuts in government spending, there will be little money available for grants or special programs for Quebec or any other special group. We would all be sharing the pain of an austerity program together, and the emphasis would be on getting the essential services delivered as economically as possible.

I do, however, recognize that there are differences, both historical and cultural, in the federal government's relationships with both Quebec and the First Nations.

There is no question that the First Nations have legitimate concerns with regard to treaty rights, and, where treaties were never signed, land claims settlements must be made. Once these concerns have been settled, however, it is important that First Nations assume control and establish self-government. If I were the prime minister I would eliminate the Department of Indian Affairs. I would promote a policy where, after settlement of land claims, natives would be citizens of Canada with the same rights and responsibilities as everyone else.

Quebec will always be different from the other provinces because of language and culture as well as its legal code. Quebeckers are proud of their struggle to assert themselves within (some might say against) the Canadian anglophone majority. The Quebec government is anxious to assume a greater control of such areas as job training, immigration, and other services that can be most efficiently delivered at a provincial level. I respect and admire Quebec's aspirations. As prime minister I would seek to adjust federal–provincial relationships to develop a model that accommodates Quebec while also offering the option for any other province to take greater control over its own destiny.

In Canada over the past fifty years, the federal government has assumed more power and control as programs and services have proliferated. It is now time to decentralize as much as possible. The days of the federal government giving major grants to provinces and other institutions is over, at least until the debt is paid down.

As we decentralize, my role as prime minister would be to emphasize and promote the common values that unite us instead of dwelling on our differences. There are always going to be differences between us as individuals, and as groups, but I would avoid categorizing people along the lines of race, creed, gender, or any other irrelevant distinction.

Lincoln said: *"You cannot further the brotherhood of man by encouraging class hatred."*

The Canadian Charter of Rights and Freedoms, the basis of our constitution, guarantees equal rights for all. Our Charter, however, does not give any individuals or groups the right to benefits paid for by others. I emphasize that families are the building blocks of a successful society, and any policy that diminishes the strength and security of the family must be challenged. Families must assume more responsibility for social assistance, for example, to support teenage mothers, the aged, and to support new immigrants that are family members.

Canadian Citizenship

Our country, as we know it, has been largely built by immigrants who have come here to find a better life. Every recent immigrant I've spoken to is proud to be a Canadian, but many of them are slightly bewildered that our policy seems to encourage them to remain "hyphenated Canadians." I believe our recent policy of promoting Canada as a "cultural mosaic" has been a major mistake. If I were prime minister, I would immediately eliminate the multicultural program and encourage all new immigrants to fit into Canadian society as soon as possible.

At present it takes only three years to qualify for Canadian citizenship, and I believe this is far too short a time to allow proper adjustment and appreciation of what it means to be a Canadian. As prime minister I would propose that citizenship be earned over a much longer period, and that it include fluency in one of Canada's official languages. I would propose that landed immigrants go through a two-year probationary period during which they would have all the basic human rights, and would have the right to work. They would not, however, have full rights of appeal to the highest court, and immigrants could be deported during this period should they commit a criminal offence. Following a two-year probation period, landed immigrant status would be granted, and only after eight full years would a new Canadian be eligible for citizenship. I do not believe eight years is an unreasonable length of time for acquiring citizenship in a country such as Canada.

Under my austerity program, and with cutbacks in all kinds of social programs, entitlements such as pensions, medicare, etc., would be earned by paying into them over the years. New Canadians would have to wait the full eight years to collect from these programs, but in the meantime, private insurance would be available. I am certain that Canadians will welcome new immigrants and, as they have in the past, assist them to integrate into Canadian society. Integration is best done on a one-on-one, neighbour-to-neighbour basis rather than by government-funded programs.

Summary

While a program of austerity is required to balance the budget and pay down our debt, and while this will undoubtedly result in short-term hardship and adjustments for almost all Canadians, there is a silver lining to the cloud. We can use this time of hardship to redefine our national goals and objectives and to develop the will to become a strong, independent country once again. I am also confident that as we attack the deficit and debt, new investment will create new jobs and a new prosperity.

I care about the future of Canada. The solutions I propose may be somewhat naive, and probably the numbers need adjusting, but I believe we need a simpler system. Our government has become overly complex and needs major reform. When you look back in our history and read the original constitution and see how the country has evolved, it becomes obvious that the pendulum must swing back towards a more self-reliant society. As it does, I am confident that the compassion and generosity of average Canadians will get us through the difficult times.

If I were prime minister, I would lead with strength, courage, and compassion, always keeping the long-term goals in mind. I would be a coach and a cheerleader at the same time, and I would try to give hope and inspiration when things were tough. I would remind Canadians to count our blessings, for we live in a great country, and with hard work, perseverance, and ingenuity, it can be the best in the world.

And always I would remember Lincoln's words: *"You cannot build character and courage by taking away man's initiative and independence."*

Notes

1. *Consensus*, National Citizens Coalition, vol. 20, no. 3 (June 1995).
2. *Reformer*, Reform Party of Canada, vol. 3, issue 2 (March 1995).
3. *Let's Talk Taxes*, Canadian Taxpayers Federation (April 21, 1995).

NINETEEN

ECONOMIC WELL-BEING AND NATIONAL UNITY: TEAM CANADA AND COACH CHRÉTIEN

• • • • • • • • • •
JAMES K. GRAY, Q.C.

*J*ames Gray is the president and chief executive officer of Calgary-based Canadian Hunter Exploration Ltd. He was recently made an Officer of the Order of Canada and he holds an Honorary Doctorate of Laws from the University of Calgary. He is a member of the Premier's Council on Science and Technology, chairman of the Science Alberta Foundation, and a member of the board of directors of the Canadian Chamber of Commerce. He is also chairman of the Canada West Foundation and a member of the board of trustees of the Fraser Institute.

TODAY, CANADA'S ECONOMIC AND POLITICAL CIRCUM-stances confront Jean Chrétien with the challenge, unparalleled in Canadian history, of resurrecting our national spirit and economy. Never before in our history have the possible costs of inaction been so frightening, nor the potential benefits of action so rewarding.

Great challenges can lift a leader to greatness or they can expose mediocrity, and, in Canada in 1995, there is no room for mediocrity. Our country's disordered economic, political, and social circumstances confront any leader with challenges that will cruelly punish mistakes or hesitations. Success will be hard bought. The consequences of failure will be the disruption, even the destruction, of our country as we have known it.

Diane McGarry, President of Xerox Canada, handily compared leadership — be it in business, charities, or politics — to the job of a coach: "Any coach's job is to assemble the best talent available, provide and communicate a winning vision and strategy and, on a daily basis, encourage team members to ensure everyone lives up to his or her potential."

As prime minister, Jean Chrétien might usefully think of himself as the national coach of a team that includes each and every individual Canadian. His job as coach requires the communication of a winning vision and strategy, the rallying of the nation, and the encouragement of team members to live up to their full potential. It will not be an easy task, but it must be done.

Economic Challenges

Pierre Trudeau was prime minister during positive economic times; the economy was growing and Canada's credit rating was first-rate. When he took office, taxes were low and the country's indebtedness was minimal. Brian Mulroney took office at a time of growth and left during a recession, leaving behind higher taxes, higher government spending, and a drastically increased debt.

Mr. Chrétien faces the problems of a declining standard of living for Canadians, slow economic growth, double-digit levels of unemployment, intensified tribalism and regionalism, and debt levels so high that they introduce an uncertainty as to whether the health of the nation's finances can or cannot be restored. Recessions repeat, and a downturn in the economy must be factored into the fiscal plan. To make matters even more challenging, the social policy framework developed in the 1960s has not accomplished its objectives and stands in dire need of fundamental reform. If Mr. Chrétien fails to rise to the challenge, the consequences of that failure will resonate from coast to coast and be noted around the world.

Unity Challenges

Pierre Trudeau faced critical challenges to the unity of the country posed by the 1970 FLQ crisis and the 1976 election of René Lévesque and the Parti Québécois. Brian Mulroney faced a politically quiescent Quebec and a co-operative federalist premier, but his attempt to bring Quebec back into the constitutional family sparked the revival of Quebec separatism and of the first separatist party to put its mark on national politics.

Prime Minister Chrétien also a faces historically significant challenge to the unity of his team. The sovereignty campaign and subsequent referendum have the potential of splitting the country. But instead of an amiable "play by the rules" democrat like René Lévesque, he faces, in Jacques Parizeau, a committed ideologue who will measure his policies not with the usual economic, political, and moral yardsticks but exclusively in terms of the profitability that they will bring to the success of his separation campaign. This, of course, is equally true of Lucien Bouchard, who attacks Canada from his position as Leader of the Official Opposition in the Canadian House of Commons.

The need for leadership is critical. Wars have been lost by a single afternoon's carelessness. Jean Chrétien is in the chilling position of being able to win the referendum for the separatists with one careless remark or ill-considered initiative.

To a disturbing degree, addressing our economic challenges intensifies the national unity problem. Stern measures to control the debt play squarely into the hands of the separatists, while the inverse would undercut the country's eroding fiscal position and give other Canadians cause to feel even more alienated from Ottawa. Compounding our concerns, all of this is occurring against the backdrop of a new era in global competition; our dependence on the American economy upon whose coattails we have ridden so comfortably for so long; and the impact of a new technological age that is undoing the basic job, economic, and lifestyle assumptions that Canadians have relied upon for decades.

The times are difficult and challenging. What should a coach for Canada be doing in what could very well be the last few minutes of the game?

The Vision

Thousands of years ago, Solomon (Proverbs 29:18) cautioned that "Where there is no vision, the people perish." The first requirement is to respond to that age-old challenge.

Canadians need a vision. They need to know who they are, where they want to go, and what is required to get there. They need to agree on their core values. This is a fundamental need that equates with clean air and pure water and must be treated with equal seriousness by government and citizens. I would push the point a notch further: after articulating the vision around which people can organize, governments must then have the discipline to step back and allow us to do things for ourselves. The coach never steps out onto the ice to make a pass or receive a body-check. That is the job of the players. That is the job of Canadians, the job of Team Canada.

There are three basic elements to the vision that I would propose Jean Chrétien provide to Canadians. They are logically separate, but they reinforce and support each other like the three legs of a stool:

1. Government must become more of a facilitator of action and less of an actor in its own right. This is the road to smaller government, which minimizes unwelcome and ineffective intervention. It ensures a government that is flexible enough to deal with the problems of accommodating to a rapidly changing world. And, at a time when Canadians are close to withdrawing their very consent to be governed, this philosophy provides responsive and sensible government.

2. The vision must empower local communities, encourage them to deal voluntarily with their own problems and to take pride in their capacity to do so. Communities should not take on this responsibility reluctantly, simply because "big government" cannot afford to do it any more, but enthusiastically, because it is just a better way of doing things. Community empowerment should be the 1990s equivalent of *maîtres chez nous* (masters in our own house). It is a notion as relevant for fishing villages in Newfoundland as it is for suburbs outside Vancouver or Montreal. It offers a meaningful focus for the human associations that surround our daily lives. It rests on a scale of human interaction that makes sense to Canadians.

3. Measures must be taken to establish a motivated, invigorated, and democratic national community, one that encourages and thrives on direct and ongoing participation, that engages the thousands of thoughtful Canadians who have "tuned out" of politics. The country needs their talents and imaginations; we cannot afford their indifference and their cynicism.

With this new vision in hand (a new playbook), how should the national coach use it to inspire Team Canada?

Leadership Styles

Prime ministerial leadership goes far beyond policy issues. It is a question of "how" as much as of "what." Jean Chrétien's leadership style will play an important role in building optimism or pessimism among Canadians, in rallying Canadians to a common vision, or in driving them into mutually hostile and isolated camps. The leader can either draw out the best in his players or drive them into bitter despair.

Pierre Trudeau is remembered as brilliant, coolly rational, but confrontational and arrogant. The first two characteristics earned him undying admiration from many Canadians, but the latter two alienated at least as many others. Elected on a wave of enthusiasm and popularity bordering on adulation, by the time he left office he had become, for many, a symbol of what they hated about Ottawa.

Brian Mulroney is described as urbane, articulate, flamboyant, and self-indulgent. Here again, if the first two qualities helped to explain his rise to power, the latter two contributed to an ever-increasing level of political cynicism among Canadians. Elected in one of the greatest electoral landslides in Canadian history, he was intensely unpopular by the time he left office.

Prime Minister Chrétien is self-deprecating, commonsensical, narrowly and fiercely partisan, and intensely loyal to his friends and historic supporters. If the latter two are the rocks on which his government could yet founder, the first two provide the springboard from which he could articulate a vision with which Team Canada can identify and rally. If the rapid fall from political grace of Trudeau and Mulroney shows how fragile such opportunities can be, the presently strong Liberal mandate shows how ready Canadians are to answer a call that they understand and believe is honest, sincere, and truthful — a call that includes austerity for the politicians equivalent to that demanded of citizens.

MPs' pensions recently became a lightning-rod for the more general issue of overall fiscal restraint in government. If I were prime minister, I would have used the issue as a symbol of my leadership. I would have eliminated pensions and encouraged all members of Parliament to provide for their own future financial security, just as increasing numbers of Canadians are doing. I mention this lost opportunity simply to draw attention to the great value of highly visible symbols of leadership.

Breaking the *Status Quo*

Our national leader must convince both his caucus and his country to break the *status quo*. The paradox of Canada is that the *status quo* is alive and well, but the *status quo* is a dead-end. In politics, the *status quo*, even with its grave flaws, continues to work reasonably well. Not so the fiscal *status quo*. It is a slippery slope to nowhere as, year after year, we spend more than we earn as a government. By a sad irony, one of the PQ's strongest arguments is the need to cut free from the mired, debt-ridden confusion of Ottawa. Even our vaunted social programs are an expensive and flawed patchwork designed for the problems of the 1950s, using the solutions of the '60s, timidly overhauled in the '70s, and yet increasingly unhelpful in the '90s. Convincing the country to break from the iron grip of the *status quo* is our prime minister's greatest challenge.

MP pension reform was an excellent vehicle upon which to base change and define new directions. There are others. Leadership in developing a new basis for the delivery of health services across this country would be one. A new concept for the organization of our armed forces would be a second. I suggest that we change the mandate of the Department of National Defence. We should focus our international commitment exclusively on peacekeeping. Forget expensive expenditures on state-of-the-art fighter planes, new submarines, tanks, etc. Let's train and equip the *best* peacekeeping force (land, air, navy) in the world. Not the biggest, just the best — an elite force of which all Canadians could be justifiably proud, an international extension, if you will, of our respected RCMP. Such a decisive action would distinguish Canada and provide a break with the past — a break from the *status quo*.

The first democratic people, the Greeks, saw government as the helmsman of a ship. How modest a vision compared with the way we look upon government today! Today, the helmsman (or government) not only wants to captain the ship but insists on providing the bunks, the meals, and the crew's medical insurance. The Canadian helmsman proposes to care for the cargo and guarantee favourable winds, a sunny day, and smooth passage. If the harbour at the end of the voyage is not to the liking of the crew, it is too easy to see it as the fault of bloated and intrusive government.

Jobs

Jean Chrétien should take every opportunity to remind Canadians that the helmsman steers and the crew runs the ship. In other words, government is incapable of raising the standard of living of Canadians and has no business in monopolizing a task it cannot do. Governments cannot create jobs, wealth, or prosperity any more than the helmsman of a ship can create good weather. When they try to do so, when they elect to bail out today's losers instead of strengthening the winners, they are, in the jargon of the sports team, playing with pick-up teams and passing over the pros.

Individual Canadians on Team Canada, those with initiative and the right opportunities, are the creators of jobs. They are the backbone of the economy, they are the basic building blocks for an improved standard of living. The team managers and coach must focus on ways of encouraging those who are creating jobs to continue to do so. At the same time, they must enable others to employ themselves and not sit and wait for someone else to create a job for them.

Empowering Communities

The leader, Jean Chrétien, must make it clear that his team will address problems from the grass roots on up. Communities must develop their own responses to problems. Volunteers must come together and organize. Other members of the community must be approached and their time, energy, and support solicited. Recruited, they must address problems in an immediate and practical way. Anyone who wishes can easily find a dozen examples from his or her own community. I would like to suggest a number from my own experience:

1. **Computers for street kids:** In Calgary, the Calgary Achievement Centre for Youth takes street kids back into the classroom to acquire literacy and numeracy skills. It uses modern computer-assisted learning techniques and co-ordinates with community employment opportunities. Although it has only been operating for a year, it has already experienced considerable success. And how did it come about? Not because of some bureaucratic decision but because an informal group from the downtown community saw what was needed and reached out to help and work with these young people.

2. **Oil workers construct a school library:** In the town of Wrentham in southern Alberta there is a new school library built jointly by the employees of a major oil company and the people of the town. The company's contribution was not in the form of a deductible charitable donation but rather in volunteer time spent doing the actual physical work of cutting the lumber and pounding nails into the boards. This corporate/community project was the result of a personal initiative by an imaginative mother.

3. **Community support for women's emergency shelter:** Several years ago, government funding for the Calgary Women's Emergency Shelter became uncertain and it was feared that some of its programs might have to close, even as the problem of family violence was becoming increasingly evident. The shelter executive responded by seeking a broader base of community support and community awareness, resulting in a hugely successful fundraising dinner. More important than the $100,000 raised was the fact that over six hundred individuals, foundations, and corporations contributed to the shelter, many for the first time. The issue of family violence received both publicity and new community support, which will translate into continuing public support in the future.

The moral of these and a thousand stories like them is that we often do not need government to do things that we as a community are capable of doing on our own. We are diminished — as a community and as individuals — when we let a remote government do something that we are perfectly capable of doing for ourselves. "Bottom-up" is simply a better way of doing things than "top-down." It is better because it provides a more effective response to immediate problems and because it can be accomplished immediately on an appropriate scale. It is better because it mobilizes and reinforces community and initiative rather than dependence.

It is also better because it is less authoritarian. To too great an extent, governments, institutions, and professionals have intruded upon the responsibility and accountability of citizens in our society. Individuals gain, in terms of self-worth and self-respect, when they are increasingly held responsible for their welfare and for the welfare of those with whom they relate.

I am reminded of this every time I see a "Neighbourhood Watch" sign on a street corner or a "Block Parent" poster in a window. I am impressed by the "Adopt-a-Highway" sign along the roadway because it tells me some family, company, or organization has taken up the responsibility for keeping the roadside clear of litter. The real essence of community is not the enjoyment of natural or man-made landmarks or some temporarily successful sports franchise but a pride in being able to work together with others for the betterment of one's fellow citizens.

Empowering communities to play a larger role in their affairs takes patience and discipline on the part of governments. Programs and solutions do not appear overnight. It takes time. Unfortunately, the practical realities of politics (i.e., elections) tempt governments into seducing voters with their own tax dollars. Our Prime Minister must discipline himself and his caucus against such behaviour.

Democracy

Our national coach, Mr. Chrétien, needs to let individual players know that they can have a direct impact on how Team Canada should work. Thousands of thoughtful Canadians have become cynical about politics. Giving them a reason to actively and directly participate in politics will require dramatic changes to the bureaucratic and partisan practices of the past several decades.

Bureaucratic structures that have imposed policy on our society for the past century have drained the vitality out of our democracy. Everywhere in the democratic world, power has flowed from elected assemblies to the political executive, and from the political executive on down to the appointed public servants. Government intervention has escalated. This trend has a thousand faces and a thousand examples; few are welcomed and many resisted everywhere. But, in past decades, the trend has become increasingly relentless as government has grown in scope, size, and complexity. Prime Minister Chrétien must pursue every option to make democracy an everyday, every-citizen process.

Some of the means of doing this are electronic. Examples include televised town-hall meetings with phone-in questions and tabulated results, documents accessible through the Internet, e-mail addresses for officials and representatives. There is nothing magic about the new technology, but it presents opportunities that must be embraced rather than resisted, with government blazing the trail rather than being dragged along it. If computers are transforming the world of business and of communication, then technology can also transform the processes of government. But the effects of technology can only be truly democratic if a wide range of citizens can take advantage of it. We should be as concerned about computer literacy as we are about the more traditional forms of literacy, and just as concerned about giving citizens access to computers and to information systems. Both "School-net," which provides students and teachers with access to the information highway, and "Community FreeNet," which provides all residents of a community with an electronic highway "learner's permit," are practical examples of what can be done.

This kind of democracy is harder work for government than the "once-every-four-years-in-the-voting-booth" style to which we have all become accustomed. But its potential benefits are tremendous. The players on Team Canada will feel more involved in the process of making decisions, and will buy into the decisions themselves, when they are convinced they are a part of a process that responds to their interests, demands, concerns, and priorities. They will become more committed to the system and the "vision" when both represent a response to their own initiative and input.

One possible future opened to us by the current technology is a participatory democracy linked through a variety of electronic channels, supplementing rather than replacing the more traditional forms of democratic participation and accountability. It has the potential to restore a vibrant sense of an interactive community in which citizenship becomes something more than a passive or reactive state. For example, New Brunswick is a leader not only in fiscal responsibility but also in using the potential of computer technology. The example is doubly reassuring and suggests that the various elements of this vision do indeed fit together rather than conflict with each other.

Here are seven practical examples of what Prime Minister Chrétien should be doing.

Lead by example

Few first ministers use their high office to limit their own perquisites. A model of the reverse is Premier Ralph Klein's elimination of MLA pensions and his 5 percent wage roll-back on his own pay package and that of his cabinet before expecting it from the rest of the public service. In this vein, Jean Chrétien has already made some positive moves, notably his personal example of being driven in a Chevy Caprice instead of a Cadillac and his relatively low-key and fiscally austere handling of the G-7 Summit in Halifax. This small beginning must be elevated into something with a much wider and more fundamental impact. It is, however, an important beginning. It signals a changed attitude.

Use the "bully pulpit"

Theodore Roosevelt once described the American presidency as a "bully pulpit" or a "splendid soap-box." The same is true of the Canadian prime ministership. The media's preoccupation with the political leaders and the "photo ops" implies a wonderful opportunity to communicate to Team Canada the dozens of success stories taking place every day in communities across the country. The Prime Minister utilized this potential during his trip to China, carefully staging the process to make points about both Canadian business opportunities and federal–provincial co-operation. This trip probably said more to Quebeckers about the value of remaining in Canada than anything else done or said by federal and provincial politicians in the past two years, and it was said better by using concrete actions rather than words.

Celebrate success

When the Prime Minister travels to any city in Canada, it would take only modest effort and research to find some local success story — a thriving new business, an unusually effective or innovative local volunteer project, a nationally renowned researcher or teacher. These deserve to be highlighted. The appropriate way to honour these individuals is not some formal presentation in Ottawa but a personal visit by the Prime Minister to the shop floor, the research lab, or the classroom.

Where the Prime Minister goes, the cameras follow. Instead of the usual "Victim of the Week," Prime Minister Chrétien could be giving the media the "Success Story of the Week." Many of these will be small-scale projects and therefore small-scale successes, but that makes them more valuable rather than less. We have to break ourselves of the habit of looking for the quick fix, the colossal mega-project that will single-handedly turn the economy around. Massive mega-projects, largely supported with public subsidies, have driven us into the fiscal swamp in which we now struggle.

Quick-fix solutions, always announced with great fanfare and celebration, create unrealistic expectations. The damage arrives with budget overruns, unanticipated losses, and missed deadlines. We have not always considered the consequences of our actions.

Yes, the Rocky Mountains, British Columbia's rain forests, the undulating, sky-filled prairies, and Prince Edward Island's beaches are all part of the wonderful landscape of which Canadians are so proud. But geography does not make a great nation. Citizens make nations. When individual citizens combine to make their community a better place in which to live, they build happy, responsible, and proud communities that result in great nations.

The implicit message to Canadians of a "Success Story of the Week" is that Canada is a vibrant and positive community full of ideas and opportunities, a community of which they are a crucial part. These success stories are a better counter-argument to separatism than threats about debt-loads or battles over balance sheets.

The light at the end of the tunnel

In order to build the kind of Canada we need tomorrow, we may need to dismantle some of the parts of the Canada we have today. This will be painful and disturbing. But it will be less so if we have some idea of why we are doing it and where we will end up. The Prime Minister must articulate this future vision.

Frank McKenna of New Brunswick is a prime example of this kind of leader. He has embarked on a deficit reduction program in a "have-not" province, but he has done so in the context of a string of governmental programs to restructure social assistance, promote small business, and make a reality out of the "information highway." Times in New Brunswick are as tough as anywhere in the country, but this has been given a positive, even exciting, slant. Prophets of doom invariably get boring even when they are right, but sharers of hope never do. The implicit message to Quebeckers is that Canada has a future that they will want to share.

Pride of citizenship

I recently had occasion to give a short talk at a citizenship court in Calgary, where fifty-seven people from twenty-two different countries were taking the oath of Canadian citizenship. I could not help being tremendously excited by their enthusiasm for Canada and its future.

We make too small a thing of these citizenship ceremonies. We take too small a pride in having a country that thousands of people want to be part of. We accept too little of the reassurance that is represented by people who think our future is worth sharing. Jean Chrétien should be using his office and high profile to remind us of this. What a dramatic statement it would make if the Prime Minister were to show up at a citizenship court in Red Deer this month, in Moncton next month, in Trois Rivières the month following, to celebrate the glory that is Canadian citizenship and the prize that it represents!

Recognize volunteer doers

One of the most undervalued assets of modern society is the willing work done by volunteers. More than one in five Canadians spend at least four hours per week on volunteer activities directed towards benefiting the community. It is important for the Prime Minister to find some practical way of acknowledging — and thereby encouraging and expanding — the enormous efforts of these invaluable activities. We use the tax system to reward charitable donations. Could we not find some way of rewarding volunteer work — rewarding people who contribute to their community by donating their time and their effort? If "less government" does not translate itself in practice into a less caring society, it will be because the communities and their network of volunteer activities fill the void and are capable of doing so more effectively than the government institutions and professionals they replace.

Encourage experimentation

Peter Drucker, one of the world's leading authorities on organizational renewal, says that one of the signs of an effective organization is that it actively plans for its own obsolescence. It anticipates what will be needed to replace itself and the essential characteristics of its replacement. It is the hallmark — and, in the modern world, the Achilles' heel — of a bureaucratic organization that it is built on exactly the opposite logic, valuing continuity over discontinuity and expansion over self-transformation. Innovation and experimentation must therefore be built into the public policy process, along with an active readiness to learn from the results (good and bad) of such attempts. One of the real strengths of a federal system is that it allows ten different provinces to tackle social assistance or medical services or advanced education in ten different ways, and then to build on the ways that demonstrably work best. Within the public service, it means making the administration of those policies that remain federal more flexible and more decentralized, and then highlighting and rewarding the successful experiments that result from that transformation. "Innovative Bureaucrat of the Month" is a less obvious idea than "Successful Businessperson of the Month," but it is another important aspect of flexible innovation that can be of lasting importance to the nation.

None of these practical examples, and none of the elements of the three-part vision for a new Canada, requires any changes to the existing constitution. There will always be an argument for changing the rules of the game, and certainly improvements can be made, but we do not need to wait for them. With leadership and imagination, the economic and unity issues of the 1990s can become the building blocks of a stronger Canada.

Conclusion

In the jargon of modern business, every organization has to have its own "mission statement." Canada's mission statement has been long buried in a constitution that few have ever read and even fewer revere. It has a prosaic tone to it. "Peace, order, and good government" does not sound like the kind of slogan calling people to the barricades. But, at a time when we can see wars on CNN almost any day, when the major urban areas of many countries seem to be sliding into chaos, and when over-reaching government seems to have condemned us and our children to a lifetime of debt, it does not sound too bad at all.

I do not need a UN survey to tell me that Canada is one of the best countries in the world in which to live. I have always known that was true. But neither do I need *The Financial Times* or *The Economist* to tell me that we have put ourselves into fiscal and political peril. That, too, I have known for a long time. What we need is a prime minister who will lead us, "coach" us if you will, by painting a more frugal, modest, and realistic vision of a smaller, more flexible government and of greater community empowerment that will enable individual Canadians to contribute to the restoration of the freedom and fiscal health of our country. Together, Canadians must be empowered to build a greater, stronger, and more generous Canada in the next century.

If I were Jean Chrétien, I would want to be remembered as a prime minister who came to office at a difficult time — possibly the only prime minister in history who could have shattered the country forever with a single major error in judgement — and who tackled the job with self-effacing humility, a sense of humour, and a matter-of-fact acceptance of priorities. I would want to have handled the downsizing of the federal government and the devolution to the provinces of most of the responsibilities for social Canada by steering the line between timidity and recklessness, and by not allowing myself to be deflected by the political posturing of separatists or special-interest critics or by the big-spending nostalgia of some members of my own caucus. I would want to have shown sympathy for those who suffered during the difficulties of the 1990s, but not to the extent of losing sight of where we, as a country, have to go. And I would want to have dispelled the separatist threat by demonstrating a clear vision of a positive future together, far better than a painful rupture, of a Canadian twenty-first century different in many ways from that of the late twentieth century but still a decent and humane country and a wonderful place to live. I would not want to be remembered as a mega-prime-minister who promised and failed to deliver. I would want to be remembered as the thoughtful and humble leader who earned the respect of the people and who inspired Canadians to love their country, help their neighbours, and join their hands in a selfless commitment to build an even finer nation.

TWENTY

A New Canadian Agenda

● ● ● ● ● ● ● ● ● ●
ARTHUR T. DOYLE

*A rthur Doyle is a Fredericton-based media and public affairs consult-
ant. His clients include corporate executives, government officials,
association professionals, and public affairs executives associated with
many of the largest organizations in North America. He is a former
newspaper publisher, national television and radio commentator, and a
bestselling author. He has written five books and numerous articles for
business and management journals.*

MY VISION OF CANADA IN THE TWENTY-FIRST CENTURY IS
that of a prosperous, self-reliant, generous, educated society, proud of
its independence, playing a significant, positive international role. As
prime minister I would promote that vision and foster the values that
would make that vision a reality.

My government would pursue policies that strengthen the family, recognizing that families flourish when people live, work, and play in safe,
healthy, and prosperous neighbourhoods and communities. It would foster
the spirit of entrepreneurship and self-reliance as a fundamental source
of our national strength. And it would make the public aware of what governments can and realistically should do with the limited resources available to them. It would protect the vulnerable in our society, particularly
the aged, the handicapped, our children, and our aboriginal peoples.

Government Reforms

As prime minister, I would recognize that, to a considerable degree,
success in achieving my government's objectives would depend on the

quality, integrity, and competence of the public service. Therefore, much attention would be given to motivating public servants and rewarding them for their performance.

Deputy ministers and other senior public servants would be given clear objectives to achieve within established time limits, and their results would be measured against those objectives. Following the New Zealand example, deputy ministers would be employed under contract for a fixed period of time. Their performance would be reviewed annually and before their contracts were renewed. They would be given sufficient authority to accomplish their jobs and would be promoted and paid according to their effectiveness. They would be encouraged to be creative and make continual improvements.

My government would seek the assistance of private sector executives to review the functions and operations of every government department and agency, on the assumption that they could all be significantly improved. As much as is practically possible, government departments would recover from other government departments the cost for their services and, in this way, they would be forced to compete with private suppliers for government business. The government would also contract out or privatize government services where it was economically and otherwise feasible. A user-pay policy would be considered for many services.

As prime minister, I would reaffirm the commitment to reduce the federal government's deficit to 3 percent of the GDP by 1996–97. I would also commit my government to balancing the budget by the year 2005.

Federal-Provincial Relations

A major challenge I would face as prime minister stems from the division of federal and provincial government responsibilities under our constitution. Without much closer federal and provincial co-operation, the Canadian Confederation will become increasingly dysfunctional. The major changes that must take place in education and health care fall under the constitutional competence of the provincial governments. Yet the national government I would lead would exercise leadership and set and maintain national standards in these two areas so that Canada could realize its national vision and become a more united nation.

For this reason, my federal government would become a closer partner with the provinces, by fostering a spirit of co-operative federalism that would allow each region to play its own unique role in the national context.

Quebec's aspirations to protect its distinct identity would be respected. But rather than seek major constitutional changes to accomplish this, my responsibility as prime minister must be, with other Canadians, to assure the Quebec people that being part of the Canadian nation is essential to their best interests, culturally and economically. I believe this will become more apparent than ever as Quebec and the rest of Canada continue to be drawn into hemispheric, indeed global, trading blocs, and as communications technology makes "the global village" even more of a reality.

Western Canada, Atlantic Canada, and Ontario, like Quebec, must be given the freedom to develop economic, cultural, and social programs tailored to their distinct aspirations and resources. The federal government I lead would transfer to the provincial governments many of the responsibilities currently shared and often duplicated in such overlapping areas as economic development, agriculture, environment, and forestry.

A more efficient and better-led and focused CBC would be given the resources it requires to foster in Canadians a sense of national identity distinct from other nations. This will be a particularly challenging task as communications technology intensifies the competition in the delivery of quality programming.

Economic Development

My government's economic-development strategy would focus much more on encouraging small business development and fostering the values of entrepreneurship, self-reliance, and risk-taking. Small businesses currently employ 40 percent of our workforce and create 80 percent of the new jobs; many of them become national and international enterprises.

To this end, my government would radically change and simplify the Income Tax Act. Its objective would be not only to collect the revenue the national government requires but to encourage economic enterprise as much as possible. We would introduce a single federal income tax rate for both corporations and individuals. It would be a "proportional" flat tax with a universal personal exemption of $15,000 and child-care deductions of $1,000 per child. This would provide a basic level of tax freedom and favour low-income families. Studies indicate that a flat-tax rate in the 20 to 25 percent range would make it revenue neutral with the present tax rate structure. This rate would be adjusted annually to generate tax revenues sufficient to meet the government's budget goals.

As prime minister I would also introduce policies to eliminate the bureaucratic confusion and frustration entrepreneurs continue to experience when they seek information, advice, and financial assistance from the federal and provincial governments. In co-operation with provincial governments, my administration would aggressively promote the recently created government "Business Service Centres" in each province. My government's trade commissioner offices would be directed to aggressively assist and encourage small business entrepreneurs to market their products and services internationally.

Education

My government would recognize that nothing will do more to improve living standards and foster national unity than ensuring that Canadians have the opportunity to acquire as much education as their abilities will allow, with education considered a lifelong continuum. Consistently, studies show us the high correlation between our education level and our living standards, our social conscience, our tolerance towards others, our health, employment prospects, and our respect for the rule of law. Education also enhances our ability to be trained and to continue learning throughout our lives.

As prime minister I would use my "bully pulpit" to encourage our public schools to place more emphasis on literacy, numeracy, and the scientific method. My government would provide resources to establish a voluntary national testing system in these areas. It would also propose to the provinces that the two levels of government jointly establish a National Institute for Teaching Excellence, which would promote ways to foster teaching excellence in public schools and universities.

Although education is a provincial responsibility, my government would provide $2 billion annually to the provinces for university funding. The necessary revenues would be generated by introducing a "Graduates Tax." All university graduates would pay an additional income tax of 1 percent, beginning at the $40,000 income level. This tax rate would increase to a maximum of 4 percent at the highest income levels and would be added to the proposed flat tax.

In return for this funding, the provincial governments would be required to introduce, within specific time-frames, a series of major reforms to make universities and their facilities more accountable for the effectiveness of their teaching professors, for the research produced, and for the value they give for the tuition and other funds they receive.

Health Care

My government would be committed to maintaining medicare. The provinces would be assured of an annual level in federal funding of $9 billion for the next several years, on the condition that the five existing principles of medicare are maintained.

Canada's hospitals and health care systems, however, are currently designed to react to health problems only when they arise — to deal with the consequences, not the major causes, of illness. Yet studies estimate that 70 percent of illnesses are preventable, and other studies show that our health care system is often used unnecessarily.

Our government would, together with the provinces, aggressively seek ways to make our health care system more effective while shifting the focus more to prevention and the promotion of healthy lifestyles. Canadians would be educated and encouraged to accept much more responsibility for the health of their communities, themselves, and their families, and to rely less on hospitals, health care professionals, and medicare.

Our government would work with the provinces to encourage the development of a more community-based health care delivery system, an expanded role for nurses, and public participation in the planning and delivery of health care services.

Our government would focus on all of the factors that determine our state of health. We would stress the importance of fostering a healthy environment in our homes, schools, workplaces, and communities. We would develop public policies that promote health in our education, justice, and taxation systems as well as in our social programs. Businesses would be encouraged to reduce pollution and the marketing of harmful products. Canadians would be educated to make wise food choices, exercise regularly, and avoid bad habits such as smoking and excessive drinking.

Social Programs

My government would maintain and improve programs that support the most vulnerable in our society, particularly our children, the aged, the handicapped, and our aboriginal peoples.

Our old age security system, based on the Old Age Pensions, the Guaranteed Income Supplement, and our Canada Pension Plan, would be maintained, but changes would be made to these programs to ensure their long-term financial viability. To this end, my government would introduce legislation to increase the eligibility age for the Old Age Pension and the Canada Pension to sixty-seven for all those who are currently under fifty years of age.

Canadians would also be encouraged to take a greater personal responsibility for financing their retirement years. Tax advantages that apply to registered retirement savings plans (RRSPs) would continue. My government would propose legislation requiring all employed Canadians to contribute 10 percent of their monthly gross earnings to an RRSP program. Those currently in a pension plan with the government or private employer could supplement those pensions to those same limits. I would point out to Canadians that the government of Chile has had a similar policy since 1981 with considerable success. Individuals, however, would only enjoy this tax benefit until they accumulate $500,000 in RRSP investments.

Although the current Canada Assistance Plan is expiring, my government would still encourage the provinces to introduce social assistance reforms and ensure national standards by attaching conditions to the new federal block-funding agreement with the provinces.

Social assistance programs would no longer provide only passive support. The goal of these programs must be to have everyone working who wants to work and is able to work. Social assistance clients must be encouraged and trained to aggressively seek and accept employment, or alternatively, to return to the classroom to learn literacy and occupational skills. Some provinces have already taken impressive steps in this direction.

No social program would be complete that did not provide child-care assistance so that low-income parents can pursue their working careers. My government would continue the current equal-funding agreement with the provinces and work with them to expand significantly the child-care spaces available in the immediate years ahead.

My government would commit itself to asserting the aboriginal peoples' right to self-government. It would work with aboriginal leaders on a plan to eventually eliminate the Department of Indian Affairs and to distribute federal funds to more effective programs designed to foster self-reliance.

International Affairs

My government would ensure that Canada continues to be a voice of reason, compassion, and goodwill on the world stage. Through international organizations, Canada would foster freer trade, promote a cleaner environment, contribute to relieving hunger in the Third World, and support collective security measures.

Our defence policy and military resources would continue to be harmonized with those of our allies, and we would continue to play a leadership role in peacekeeping within the United Nations. We would, however, invest in defence technology that would also serve our particular needs, such as patrolling our coastlines and the northern territories.

Conclusion

I know that in the concluding years of the twentieth century paradigm shifts in thinking must take place about what governments should and should not do. As prime minister I would be leading the public, and particularly the public service, in an era of dramatic change, knowing that many of the necessary changes would foment controversy, resistance, and a sense of insecurity.

To be effective, my government would have to respond to the public's growing insistence on more accountability from public servants, institutions, and elected officials, and to its desire to be consulted, listened to, and to participate in public policy-making. Canadians would be informed in clear, straightforward language of what the government is doing and intends to do as it affects their lives. I would strive to make the government process more transparent, and Canadians would have an opportunity to debate fully all of the significant decisions that lead to new legislation, including the budget, prior to the decisions being made. There would be very few surprises when my government made announcements.

The greater public participation would not mean that my government would pander to the growing number of special interest groups and their increasingly strident voices. As prime minister I would consult, be willing to take advice, and listen. Then I would make each decision following input according to my best, informed judgement, in the context of our goals and values.

As prime minister, I would use my office to educate, to inform, and to challenge Canadians, for when all is said and done, it is they who must do the real work.

In governing, I would always be mindful of the reality that the great political leaders have not depended simply on regulations and legislation to make their national vision a reality.

"A leader is best," according to the sixth-century-BC Chinese philosopher Lao-Tzu, "when people barely know that he exists. When his work is done, his aim fulfilled, they will say, 'We did this ourselves.'"

MAGNA FOR CANADA
SCHOLARSHIP FUND

IN 1995, MAGNA INTERNATIONAL, INC., ALLOCATED ONE million dollars to establish the **Magna for Canada Scholarship Fund**, an annual awards program for Canadian college and university students. The program is designed to provide a national forum for new and innovative ideas with a view to creating a more prosperous country.

The Scholarship Fund will provide cash awards each year to ten regional winners from across the country, one of whom will be selected as the national champion. In addition to the student winners, up to ten recognized Canadians will also submit proposals in the Invitational category, one of whom will be declared the Invitational winner.

The awards program is sponsored by Magna International, Inc., Canada's largest supplier of automotive systems and components, and the Fair Enterprise Institute, a non-political and non-profit organization founded to improve Canadian living standards.

For more information on the **Magna for Canada Scholarship Fund**, including details on how to participate in this year's competition, please call 1-800-976-2462 or write to the following address:

Magna for Canada Scholarship Fund
36 Apple Creek Boulevard
Markham, Ontario
L3R 4Y4